D1518428

CAREERS IN THE US ARMED FORCES

CAREERS IN THE US COAST GUARD

Judy Silverstein Gray and Taylor Baldwin Kiland

Enslow Publishing
101 W. 23rd Street
Suite 240
New York, NY 10011
USA

enslow.com

Published in 2016 by Enslow Publishing, LLC.
101 W. 23rd Street, Suite 240, New York, NY 10011

Library of Congress Cataloging-in-Publication Data
Gray, Judy Silverstein.
 Careers in the US Coast Guard / Judy Silverstein Gray and Taylor Baldwin Kiland.
   pages cm. — (Careers in the US Armed Forces)
 Includes bibliographical references and index.
 Summary: "Describes career opportunities in the US Coast Guard"—Provided by publisher.
 Audience: Grades 7-8.
 ISBN 978-0-7660-6945-9
 1. United States. Coast Guard—Vocational guidance—Juvenile literature. 2. United States. Coast Guard—
Juvenile literature. I. Kiland, Taylor Baldwin, 1966- II. Title.
 VG53.G728 2015
 363.28'602373—dc23
                          2015015138

Printed in the United States of America

Portions of this book originally appeared in the book *The U.S. Coast Guard and Military Careers*.

Photo Credits: ©AP Images, pp. 12, 35; Christine Yarusi, p.1 (series logo); Coast Guard photo by BM1 Peter
Rossi/DVIDS, p.62; Corey Sipkin/NY Daily News Archive via Getty Images, p.10; Courtesy of the US Coast
Guard Art Program, Washington D.C., p.21; DoD photo by Fireman Adam Campbell, US Coast Guard, p.60;
Library of Congress, Prints and Photographs Division, p.16; Mike Hayes/Wikimimedia Commons/Ida Lewis
001.jpg/public domain, p.24; ml/Shutterstock.com, p.1 (top left); PA1 CHUCK KALNBACH, US Navy/
Wikimedia Commons/Harbor patrol during Operation Desert Shield.jpg/public domain, p. 102; PathDoc/
Shutterstock.com, p. 1 (top right); Petty Officer 2nd Class Eric J. Chandler/Wikimedia Commons/A US Coast
Guard MH-65 Dolphin helicopter with Air Station Barbers Point practices surf search and rescue techniques in
Haleiwa, Hawaii, Jan. 18, 2013 130118-G-ZQ587-002.jpg/public domain, p.104; Petty Officer 2nd Class Tim
Kuklewski/US Coast Guard via Getty Images, p.7; Photo by Journalist 2nd Class Josh Glassburn, USN, p.110;
Steve Cukrov/Shutterstock.com (chapter openers); USCG Historian's Office, pp.28,31,33,36,40,50,86,88; US
Coast Guard photo, pp.23,55,65; US Coast Guard photo/DVIDs, pp. 42,106; US Coast Guard photo by Chief
Warrant Officer Donnie Brzuska, p.73; U.S Coast Guard photo by Fireman David Segal, p.64; US Coast Guard
photo by Lt. James Cullen/Wikimedia Commons/USCG RAID.jpg/public domain, p.80; US Coast Guard
photo by PA1 Rob Wyman/DVIDS, p.100; US Coast Guard photo by PA3 Aida Cabrera/DVIDS, p.107; US
Coast Guard photo by Public Affairs Specialist 3rd Class Kelly Newlin, p.70; US Coast Guard photograph by
Petty Officer 1st Class Adam Eggers, p.93; US Coast Guard photo by Petty Officer 1st Class Andrew Kendrick
, p.46; US Coast Guard photo by Petty Officer 1st Class Henry, p.112; US Coast Guard photo by Petty Officer
1st Class George Degener, p.98;US Coast Guard photo by Petty Officer 1st Class Krystyna Hannum, p.68; US
Coast Guard photo by Petty Officer 1st Class Shawn Eggert, p.109; US Coast Guard photo by Petty Officer
2nd Class Michael Anderson, p.79;US Coast Guard photo by Petty Officer 2nd Class Annie Elis/Wikimedia
Commons/Coast Guard Cadet Christopher Salinas marches down 5th Ave.jpg/public domain, p.83; US Coast
Guard photo by Petty Officer 3rd Class Tara Molle/DVIDS, p.49; US Coast Guard Petty Officer 2nd Class
Thomas M. Blue/flickr.com;6950610528_8343aeb514_b.jpg/United States government work, p.96; US Coast
Guard photo by 2nd Class Cadet Samuel Keith/DVIDS, p.75; US Coast Guard photo by Petty Officer 3rd Class
David R. Marin, p.67;US Coast Guard photo by Petty Officer 3rd Class Victoria Bonk, pp.92; US Coast Guard/
Wikimedia Commons/Defense.gov photo essay 100421-G-0000L-003.jpg/public domain, p.58; US Coast
Guard/Wikimedia Commons/VADM Vivien Crea official portrait.jpg/public domain, p.90;

Cover: ml/Shutterstock.com (top left); PathDoc/Shutterstock.com (top right); US Coast Guard Photo by Petty
Officer 2nd Class Sabrina Laberdesque (bottom); Christine Yarusi (series logo).

CONTENTS

Acknowledgements From Judy Silverstein Gray

With great love for my my parents who shared their love of oceans and who read us stories that fueled our imaginations and lifelong passion for reading. They made excursions to bookstores and the library into adventures, ensuring no ride in the car or camping trip was taken without a stack of good books. To this day, it makes me smile to reach way up on our home library shelves for an oversized and antique version of a tale of the sea with hand-cut engravings of sailing ships and ancient mariners I recall thumbing through as a family. I am also grateful to my brother Mark, who tells a narrative better than anyone I know and who shared many childhood adventures at the water's edge. Finally, it is dedicated to my incredibly talented and kind husband Rich, who chooses words and books carefully and with great respect. I have shared my love of sea stories with each of them. These are the people who have shared my passion for service above self, my love of a good story, and my connection to the sea.

HOVERING HELPERS

A desperate distress call came in just before dawn on October 29, 2012, to the Coast Guard Air Station Elizabeth City, in North Carolina. The tall ship HMS *Bounty*, a replica of the ship featured in the story *Mutiny on the Bounty*, was caught in the middle of a treacherous storm. Called a "super-storm," Hurricane Sandy had affected twenty-four states and had the highest storm surge ever recorded. As the *Bounty* tried navigating around the hurricane, she lost propulsion and the ship's generator failed, causing it to take on water. That proved too much for the crew, and they were forced to abandon ship.

As Sandy barreled up the Northeast corridor after initially forming as a tropical wave slashing at the Caribbean, the crew hailed the search-and-rescue experts on their radio.

Petty Officers Randy Haba and Daniel Todd, who worked as Aviation Survival Technicians, were sent to the scene with crews on two rescue helicopters. Flying through the dangerous outer bands of the hurricane, they were buffeted around by torrential rains and strong winds. As they arrived to rescue the crew, they found the *Bounty* partially submerged and surrounded by debris and several life rafts. The rescue swimmers went to work.

Battling strong currents, 18-foot waves, driving 40 mile-per-hour winds and rain, they swam towards the life rafts. Todd described it as being like "swimming in a washing machine."[1] One by one, the duo pulled survivors from life rafts over to the waiting rescue basket dangling from the helicopter hovering above. Swimming back and forth from the life rafts to the basket, they fended off the effects of fatigue and cold. Through perseverance and with great skill they safely rescued fourteen crew members. The two men were awarded the International Maritime Organization (IMO) Award for Exceptional Bravery at Sea.

Hurricane Sandy killed nearly 150 people and the damage was estimated at $65 billion. The only hurricane that caused more damage was Hurricane Katrina in 2005.

Hurricane Katrina

In 2014, the US Coast Guard rescued more than 20,000 people.[2] Coast Guard helicopter crews routinely meet unusual challenges during rescues. In stormy weather, they often face unexpected challenges, relying upon ingenuity and creativity and the experience of the entire crew. Nowhere was that more evident than in New Orleans during Hurricane Katrina in 2005. Rescuers usually hoist people from the water

Coast Guard officers rescued crewmembers of the HMS *Bounty* after receiving a distress call. The craft was submerged in the Atlantic Ocean during Hurricane Sandy and its crew was in serious danger.

Hoax Calls

Sometimes calls that come into the Coast Guard requesting assistance are false. That means the Coast Guard sends its crews on hoax calls, which prevent them from responding to true emergencies. Back in 1990, the Coast Guard began keeping statistics on hoax calls and, in that year, Coast Guard crews responded 205 times to false alarms. Unfortunately, this number has increased steadily every year.

Each year, hundreds of thousands of dollars are wasted on hoax calls and valuable time that could be spent responding to the real emergency calls is wasted. It's important to know those found guilty of a hoax call can be imprisoned for up six years, criminally fined up to $250,000 and may have to reimburse the Coast Guard for the amount spent searching unnecessarily. But you can help by doing the right thing. If you hear a hoax call, or know about someone who called in false information, call your local US Coast Guard unit.

about fifty feet above the water into their aircraft. Yet during Hurricane Katrina, helicopter crews had to hover high above rooftops and near dangerous power lines executing hoists that were longer than 120 feet. In spite of the intense manuevering required, helicopter crews were a welcome sight for those whose homes were surrounded by water, because they provided a safe, if unexpected, return to dry ground.

Petty Officer Josh Mitcheltree had worked as a rescue swimmer in Alaska and had dangled from a hovering helicopter above the sea countless times. But as a twenty-three-year-old, the North Carolina native tackled his toughest mission on August 30, 2005. That was just after Hurricane Katrina ravaged the Gulf Coast, submerging entire neighborhoods, killing hundreds of people, and stranding thousands more. No strangers to treacherous weather and unpredictable storms, Coast Guard crews faced new challenges with this dangerous hurricane.

As Petty Officer Mitcheltree looked out the window of his HH-60 Jayhawk helicopter, the earth below him looked nearly flattened. The crew grew silent as they flew along the coast from Mobile, Alabama, to New Orleans, Louisiana. They saw leveled buildings and uprooted ancient oak trees. They heard the radio crackle with descriptions of the storm's historic and shocking path of destruction. Mitcheltree saw water where city buildings once stood.

The rescue swimmer had heard about the groups of desperate people anxiously awaiting rescue. Facing 100-degree summer heat, difficult rescues from slippery rooftops, and the dangers of tangled power lines, Mitcheltree starte planning. "I joined the Coast Guard to help people, and being a rescue swimmer seemed like the most hands-on people kind of job," he said. "In New Orleans, it was no different but it was the hugs afterwards that made it all worthwhile. I was doing something that seemed to make a difference."[3] Many Coast Guard crews who worked in the Gulf Coast region after Hurricane Katrina felt the same way.

Early that first morning, Mitcheltree had prepared for a long day and saw a crowd of people frantically waving from steep rooftops. Arriving on scene, things seemed chaotic as uprooted trees and severed branches covered virtually every

People were not the only ones in need of rescuing during Hurricane Katrina. Here, a volunteer saves a dog from the flooded streets.

surface. The force of gale winds upended shopping carts and pieces of vehicles had landed in treetops at odd angles. Mitcheltree recalled a two-year-old girl who cried as he placed her carefully in the helicopter basket that would lift her to safety. As he reassured the frightened child who had been separated from her mother, she pulled herself close into his body and closed her eyes, clutching him tightly. Rescues were helping bring storm victims to safer and drier ground, In fact, during the ten days after Hurricane Katrina hit the Gulf Coast, the Coast Guard rescued thirty-three thousand people. Helicopters from different agencies circled the skies with a deafening noise, as the winds shook the basket with the child inside. Once the child was reunited with her mother in the helicopter, Mitcheltree felt a surge of emotions: "I just kept thinking of how someone I rescued reminded me of someone in my own family," he said.[4] In just one week, Mitcheltree completed 138 rescues. His efforts earned him a Presidential Citation and a call from President George Bush. "That was pretty fun," he said. "I felt like the winner of the Super Bowl. The President thanked me and told me he appreciated the work I was doing."[4] Mitcheltree was also awarded the Air Medal for his heroics.

Like many rescue swimmers, Mitcheltree is humble. He is quick to deflect any credit to others and said the Coast Guard is full of many heroes and heroines. "The best thing about the Coast Guard is there are so many people doing a lot of good things."[5] On the scene in New Orleans, he recalled advice from a former supervisor who said a rescue swimmer must be the calming factor in the middle of chaos. That advice came in handy as Mitcheltree and other crewmembers demonstrated their confidence and training. Though the

The Coast Guard was called on to rescue abandoned New Orleans residents as floodwaters rose after Hurricane Katrina struck.

circumstances were unusual, Mitcheltree said the hurricane operations went smoothly because skilled people worked as a team, despite the wind, high temperatures, and tough challenges related to longer than usual hoists. Their work in New Orleans showed the world that the Coast Guard crews are world-class lifesavers.

Specialized training is emphasized so that Coast Guard crews remain ready to rescue people whose lives are in danger. However, they also perform homeland-security patrols and keep an eye out for polluters. And although the Coast Guard is the smallest of the five armed forces, it has exclusive authority to patrol the waters of the United States. With a diverse and varied history spanning more than two centuries, today's Coast Guard is a blend of other agencies that formerly existed. Yet, traditions of lifesaving and maintaining safety in ports remain as important as the Coast Guard's search-and-rescue efforts during stormy weather.

TWO CENTURIES, MANY MISSIONS

Since the earliest days of our nation's history, the United States Coast Guard has helped secure our ports, protect trade, and has been safeguarding life and property at sea for more than 225 years. The history of the Coast Guard has often reflected the growth of maritime interests at home and overseas. Many of the original duties of the service are still an essential piece of homeland and port-security duties today. As the oldest continuous maritime service, the Coast Guard once served as our country's navy. As early as the 1790s, it quarantined ports during outbreaks of diseases, such as yellow fever. The Coast Guard has also provided crews and ships in support of the US Navy during times of war.

Fighting Pirates

The United States struggled to find ways to generate money to pay off a growing national debt after the Revolutionary

War. The first secretary of the treasury, Alexander Hamilton, created a plan to tax imported goods brought into American ports by foreign ships. However, piracy on the high seas and dangerous weather posed a simultaneous threat to commerce and the safety of American ports. Life at sea was often hazardous.

Raised on the island of Nevis in the Caribbean, Hamilton was familiar with smuggling ships that avoided paying taxes. He knew that piracy interfered with trade and border security.

In 1787, Hamilton was hatching a plan to create a maritime service with varied capabilities. He once wrote (in *The Federalist Papers, No. 12*), "A few armed vessels, judiciously stationed at the entrances of our ports, might at a small expense be made useful sentinels of our laws." Recognizing the need for patrols, Hamilton created America's Revenue Cutter Service. By establishing the service, Hamilton ensured the collection of taxes that would help generate funds for the new nation. The Tariff Act of August 4, 1790, called for a fleet of ten cutters.[1] (A cutter is a ship that is sixty-five feet or longer.) Often considered the father of the Coast Guard, he also provided one hundred people to assist in tariff collection on goods entering American ports. They also kept an eye out for security threats to our ports, thus kicking off a tradition of service to our nation that included safety and security at sea.

Sometimes called the Revenue Marine, the service operated as a maritime police force protecting America's coasts. Each ship had a crew of ten, who earned about twelve dollars each month. Hamilton also lobbied Congress to give each man a military rank.

Crews were comprised of those with sailing experience and were well-educated in our nation's laws, conducting

Alexander Hamilton established America's Revenue Cutter Service, a fleet responsible for port tax collection and safety patrol of the nation's ports.

inspections of documents such as cargo lists (manifests). They often seized vessels found in violation of the law. The vital missions given to those first Revenue Cutter sailors meant their ships had to be both quick enough to chase larger vessels at sea and nimble enough to maneuver through shallow and busy ports and harbors. Some ships were appropriately named *Diligence* and *Vigilant* for their efforts standing watch, while others were named for Revolutionary War heroes such as Adjutant General Alexander Scammell. Still others were named for the original thirteen states, such as the *Massachusetts*. Some of these original vessel names chosen in the early days of the Revenue Cutter Service are still used by the Coast Guard on newer versions.

The first commissioned officer of the Revenue Cutter Service was Hopley Yeaton of New Hampshire, who had served in the Continental Navy during the Revolutionary War. Appointed on March 21, 1791, by President George Washington, Yeaton was named "Master of a Cutter in the Service of the United States for the Protection of Revenue" and was assigned to the 57-foot schooner *Scammel*.[2]

First Test in Combat: The Quasi War (1798–1800)

Although the Revenue Cutter captains had a military rank, it was not until 1798 that it proved its battle readiness during the Quasi War with France. Called the "Quasi" War because it was undeclared and fought almost entirely at sea, the conflict erupted after the French seized American ships in protest of trade between the United States and Great Britain. In response, the United States Congress authorized President John Adams to arm and acquire up to twelve vessels, canceling

The US Lighthouse Service

Safeguarding life and property at sea has been a longstanding skill mastered by Coast Guard crews. There were very few buildings onshore and much of the new nation's coast was rocky. Night passage by ship could be dangerous, especially in windy and stormy weather. The American colonies established lighthouses in 1716 to help light the way and provide safer passage. Some used primitive lanterns lit by candles or whale oil, and were manned by brave volunteers. By 1812, lighthouse keepers were assigned to lighthouses, often using whale oil to ensure the light burned continuously through the night. After 1822, some lighthouses were fitted with a Fresnel lens to magnify or bend the light, and provide better illumination for ships crossing over rocky channels.

Lighthouse keepers often had to summon volunteers to help rescue mariners at sea. Tales of brave lighthouse keepers are a rich part of the Coast Guard's courageous and exciting search-and-rescue legacy and some of the Coast Guard's cutters bear their names. Interestingly, many women often served dutifully, as did war veterans. The United States Lighthouse Service, formed in 1910, officially became part of the Coast Guard in 1939.

all treaties with her former ally. During the Quasi War, the Revenue Cutter Service saw her cutter *Pickering* capture ten ships. However, the war ended in 1800 when French piracy declined and a treaty was signed.

The First "Brown-Water" War: The War of 1812

In the early 1800s, the United States went to war with Great Britain for a second time. British vessels were disrupting American shipping. In what became known as the War of 1812, the Navy sought the assistance of the Revenue Cutter Service because she had a fleet of ships that could navigate in shallow-water ports. This war began a long history of fighting "brown water" wars—which are fought closer to shore.

On the night of June 12, 1813, the Revenue Cutter *Surveyor*, with her crew of sixteen, was captured by the British frigate, HMS *Narcissus* after fierce hand-to-hand combat in the Chesapeake Bay. The courage and expertise of Revenue Cutter crews had become legendary and the official and colorful battle account said:

> *Although outnumbered and surrounded by the enemy, the crew did not flinch, contesting the deck with stubborn courage in response to ringing appeals from Captain Travis, who did not surrender his vessel until further resistance would have resulted in useless and wanton shedding of blood.*[3]

The Revenue Cutter Service also became the first US military service to capture a British ship when the *Vigilant* captured the British ship *Dart* on October 4, 1813.

First Coast Guard Commandant Captain Ellsworth Price Bertholf

Captain Ellsworth Price Bertholf led a few courageous rescues. As part of the Overland Expedition of 1897–1898, his crew successfully rescued a fleet of 273 whalers trapped by ice near Point Barrow, Alaska. Creativity, flexibility, adaptability, and physical stamina—all considered good characteristics for those serving in the Coast Guard—were the hallmarks of his work. He led a similar and challenging rescue-and-relief mission in Russia. In his day, Bertholf and his team were awarded the Congressional Medal of Honor for their courageous efforts rescuing mariners.

In 1895, Bertholf, became the first Revenue Cutter officer to attend the Naval War College in Newport, Rhode Island. He had also proudly led the Revenue Cutter Service and oversaw development of an ice patrol, after the *Titanic* sunk after hitting an iceberg. Beginning in 1911, Bertholf served as commandant of the Revenue Cutter Service, navigating the small service through political storms that continually threatened to shut down its existence.

In 1915, when the Coast Guard was formally created, Bertholf was named first commandant of the Coast Gu ard. His vision of a maritime military service with many important missions and jobs continues to endure and inspire Coast Guard leaders. In fact, the Coast Guard's first National Security Cutter, *Bertholf,* was christened on November 11, 2006, in honor of this courageous and visionary Coast Guard leader.

The Revenue Cutter Service craft *Vigilant* captured the British *Dart* during the War of 1812, the first capture by a US service military craft. This feat helped establish the traditions of today's Coast Guard.

Fighting the Seminole Indians and the Mexicans

In 1832, the secretary of the treasury ordered the Revenue Service to assist mariners in the icy winter months. By 1837, lifesaving became a vital and core mission and the foundation of work performed by the modern-day Coast Guard crews. From 1836 to 1839, the fleet was called up to help fight the Seminole Indian Wars on inland rivers and waterways in Florida. Seminoles were attacking American settlements on their former lands.

Lifesavers

At a time when sailors navigated using simple instruments and the moon, hazards at sea jeopardized the lives of mariners. That led to the creation of volunteer lifesaving forces. In Massachusetts, lifesaving stations stocked life jackets, life cars (gear and pulley systems), and occasionally a horse-drawn cart and small lifesaving boats. By 1848, various stations dotted the Atlantic and Pacific coasts, the Gulf of Mexico, and the Great Lakes to assist mariners. By 1854, a full-time station keeper was paid by the government.

In 1871, Sumner Kimball became Chief of the Treasury Department's Revenue Marine Division. Kimball convinced Congress to appropriate $200,000 to operate stations. The Secretary of the Treasury was also allowed to employ full-time crews, and in 1878, a network of life saving stations were formally organized into the Life-Saving Service.

On January 28, 1915, President Woodrow Wilson signed the "Act to Create the Coast Guard," merging the Life-Saving Service with the Revenue Cutter Service to create the modern-day Coast Guard. By the time the act was signed, a network of more than 270 stations provided service in areas near the Atlantic Ocean, Pacific Ocean, coasts along the Gulf of Mexico, and the Great Lakes.[4] This provided an important service for mariners and commercial shipping.

Sumner Kimball (1834–1923) transformed the scattered, volunteer-run lifesaving stations into a well-trained, well-equipped organization.

In the Vanguard: Lighthouse Keeper Ida Lewis

Credited with saving at least eighteen lives, Idawalley Zorada Lewis, along with her mother, tended the Lime Rock Lighthouse in Newport, Rhode Island. The two took over for Ida's father when he suffered a disabling stroke in 1857, when Ida was not quite fifteen years old. She served until her death on October 24, 1911.[5] President Ulysses S. Grant visited her after word of her courageous and heroic rescues eventually made it to the White House. Notably, she became the official keeper of the Lime Rock Lighthouse In 1879, forty-five years later Lime Rock Lighthouse was renamed Ida Lewis Lime Rock Lighthouse, making it the first and only lighthouse named for a keeper. In 1995, the Coast Guard named a buoy tender stationed at Newport, Rhode Island, in her honor.

Ida Lewis

The Coast Guard's fleet provided invaluable support to the US Marine Corps by providing shallow-draft vessels that could blockade the coasts and conduct amphibious landings. These ships also contributed to the success of shore battles during the Mexican–American War (1846–1848), which was fought over a land dispute in what is now Texas.

The Civil War and the Spanish-American War

In the early nineteenth century, the Revenue Cutter Service also intercepted ships participating in the slave trade. Outlawed in 1808, African slaves were often chained in the lower decks of ships coming to America. The conflict that began over slavery soon led to the Civil War.

In South Carolina, the cutter *Harriet Lane* fired the first shots of the Civil War, on April 11, 1861. When President Abraham Lincoln was assassinated in 1865, Revenue Cutter personnel were also ordered to search ships for assassins.

During the Spanish-American War, the Revenue Cutter Service expanded their protective duties beyond America's coastline, joining their Navy counterparts in 1898 to blockade Havana Harbor in Cuba. The United States had gone to war with Spain after a US Navy ship, the USS *Maine*, exploded in the harbor. During the war, the Revenue Cutter Service also manned lifesaving stations as observation posts, providing a critical and useful line of homeland defense.

When President Woodrow Wilson signed the "Act to Create the Coast Guard," combining the Life-Saving Service and the Revenue Cutter Service, it opened a new chapter in the first armed force known as the Coast Guard.

CHANGING WITH THE TIMES

As America ventured into the international arena, she became a world power in the early twentieth century, facing new military challenges.

The First World War

In April 1917, when five American merchant ships were sunk by German submarines off the American coast, President Woodrow Wilson asked Congress to declare war to make the world "safe for democracy."[1] As during previous wars, the Coast Guard was moved under the control of the Navy. To safeguard the security of our ports, the Coast Guard seized enemy merchant ships in US harbors, quickly regaining control of its homeland waterways. Five Coast Guard cutters—the *Tampa, Seneca, Yamacraw, Ossipee, Algonquin,* and *Manning*—also sailed to Gibraltar to join the Atlantic fleet, earning high praise for their work safeguarding ships.

However, despite her successful escort of more than 350 vessels, the cutter *Tampa* was unexpectedly struck by a torpedo and sunk. It was a tragic loss and the largest single seagoing loss of American life during World War I.[2] Crews assigned to the *Tampa, Seneca,* and *Ossipee* protected 1,526 merchant ships in 280 convoys, while the *Seneca* rescued 139 survivors from four ships that had been torpedoed.[3]

Law Enforcement

After World War I, Coast Guard crews patrolled US and Alaskan coasts, performing search-and-rescue missions with only 4,000 members. In 1919, after the Eighteenth Amendment was passed prohibiting the manufacture, sale, or transportation of alcohol, Coast Guard missions were expanded to include enforcement of smuggling laws. In 1922, the service rescued three thousand mariners, but rumrun-ners posed a challenge that had to be tackled.

Although the Coast Guard had a staffing shortage, crews in 1927 captured the treacherous Horace Alderman, known as the Gulf Stream Pirate, thirty-five miles off the coast of Florida. While several Coast Guardsmen were transporting a Secret Service agent to Bimini, Alderman attacked. A gory shoot-out left two Coast Guardsmen and one FBI agent dead. Alderman was hanged for murder on the high seas on August 17, 1929, at Coast Guard Base #6 near Fort Lauderdale. A confirmed smuggler, Alderman is the only person hanged by the Coast Guard.[4]

Coast Guard Aviation

During the 1920s and 1930s, the Coast Guard rapidly expanded its aviation program, growing it from a single,

Coast Guard cutter *Tampa* was sunk during World War I after escorting more than 350 US vessels to safety.

borrowed seaplane in 1920 to fifty aircraft, seven air stations, and two air detachments in 1938.[5] Daily air patrols of Gloucester Harbor, Massachusetts, helped thwart rumrunners and the development of amphibious aircraft helped rescue mariners in distress.

In 1935, the United States passed the Neutrality Act to provide aid to our allies and prevent arms and ammunition from reaching the hands of enemies. While enforcing the Neutrality Act, the Coast Guard seized sixty-four German and Japanese ships in US ports.[6]

Icebreaking Duty

A vital component of the US economy is linked to the free flow of commerce and clear shipping lanes to allow imported and exported goods, such as fuel and oil, safe passage through our ports. From clearing harbor ice in eastern seaports to icebergs in Alaska, the Coast Guard's icebreaking mission keeps commerce moving. The cutters *Bear, Corwin,* and *Thetis* were built to withstand ice and help rescue whalers and fishermen. However, the Coast Guard's first true icebreakers were built in 1926.

Today, the Coast Guard oversees all icebreaking duties for the military as they steam through hundreds of miles of ice with specially constructed ships.

The Second World War

When the Japanese surprise attacked an American fleet in Pearl Harbor, Hawaii, on December 7, 1941, the Coast Guard ships *Taney, Kukui, Reliance, Walnut,* and *Tiger* were part of the military response. As an onslaught of Japanese fighter jets flew overhead, American crews courageously fired back to thwart further destruction. When the Japanese withdrew, the Coast Guard secured the entrance to Honolulu harbor.

After Pearl Harbor, the United States entered the war, and the Coast Guard found itself transferred once again to the Department of the Navy. Coast Guard crews boarded the

Norwegian fishing vessel *Buskoe,* in Greenland, discovering radio equipment. Her crew revealed it was intended to establish a station for Germany.

In 1942, Douglas Munro, a twenty-two-year-old Coast Guard signalman from Elam, Washington, took charge of a wooden Higgins Boat to help with an amphibious Marine Corps landing. Maneuvering his boat between enemy fire and troops, Munro worked tirelessly to provide enough cover to rescue the Marines. Returning one last time to ensure the safe rescue, Munro was shot and died of head wounds. He remains the Coast Guard's only Medal of Honor recipient. Munro's medal commends his work for "extraordinary heroism and conspicuous gallantry in action above and beyond the call of duty."[7] The Coast Guard Cutter *Munro* is named in his honor.

The Coast Guard performed many critical missions during this war. More than eight hundred cutters and one hundred eighty thousand people conducted convoy escorts. Coast Guardsmen also played a vital role. The Coast Guard played a critical part getting landing troops ashore at Normandy, France, on D-Day. The Battle of Normandy played a significant role helping the United States and its allies in the fight against Germany. The Coast Guard provided expert boat-handling expertise for troops battling in the Pacific, played a critical role in most major World War II amphibious landings, harnessing its boat-handling expertise and demonstrating skill in search-and-rescue missions.

On February 23, 1945, in Iwo Jima, Bob Resnick of New York faithfully stood deck watch and also supplied the American flag and a twenty-one-foot steamfitter's pipe for use as a flagpole to the Marines.[8] As they struggled to hoist

A landing craft infantry amphibious ship transports troops to Utah Beach for the Battle of Normandy on D-Day.

it above the infamous volcanic sands atop Mount Suribachi, Associated Press photographer Joe Rosenthal captured the moment in a photograph for the Associated Press. The hoisting of the flag after days of treacherous combat on foreign soils immortalized at the Marine Corps War Memorial in Arlington, Virginia.

Back on the eastern seaboard of the United States, the cutters *Bedloe* and *Jackson* patrolled the coast of North Carolina, searching for German U-boats, or submarines. While trying to rescue a torpedoed ship, both were sunk in the Great Atlantic Hurricane of 1944, leaving only nineteen survivors, including William Ruhl, who escaped from the engine room of the *Jackson*. "I was proud to serve my country and I learned to love the Coast Guard," said Ruhl, a Pennsylvania native, who scoffed at the notion that he is a hero.[9] It is these important sacrifices in a small military service that made a difference in the security of our waterways.

During the war, lighthouses and aids to navigation were maintained, key sea channels were cleared of ice, and beach patrols ensured spies did not penetrate our ports. Using dogs and horses, the Beach Patrol kept a lookout on 95,000 miles of our vulnerable coastline, protecting residents from possible enemies. Coast Guard Captains of the Port ensured cargo was safely transported, laying down the groundwork for port, cargo, container, and marine safety. These expanded duties prompted the Coast Guard to not only create a women's reserve (SPARs), but also to rely on the draft to fill personnel shortages, and to formally integrate African Americans into Coast Guard service.

The USCGC *Northland* patrolled the waters off of Greenland during World War II. The ship performed the firs US naval capture of the war by seizing a German boat. During the war, *Northland* performed missions to destroy German radio and weather stations around Greenland.

Women in the Coast Guard

The Coast Guard Women's Reserve was created in 1941 and was called "SPAR." The word SPAR stands for "Semper Paratus, Always Ready" and is the Coast Guard motto. A women's reserve helped fill critical shore jobs left vacant when men left for war. Between 1942 and 1946, more than ten thousand women between twenty and thirty-six years of age joined the SPARs. From secretarial to mechanical duties, women filled roles so that male workers could serve overseas.

Lorraine Dieterle was one of many who performed distinguished services. Dieterle served as a photographer, earning the nickname "Shutterbug." "My job was to teach the men combat photography, how to stay alive with a camera and a gun on their back, how to block out their cameras, how to mix developer with seawater, how to go through the jungles and how to photograph the landings on D-Day."[10]

Prior to her death on the Coast Guard's birthday, August 4, 2013, Dieterle was instrumental in ensuring the Women in Military Service Memorial at Arlington National Cemetery properly represented the Coast Guard and the service of all women. Dieterle literally broke through every barrier to women, often working on the frontlines to document and help others document combat action during World War II.

SPAR Lorraine Dieterle performed critical service during World War II; she trained combat cameramen how to develop film with seawater and how to capture action shots.

USCGC *Spencer* was involved in combat action in both the Atlantic and Pacific theaters of World War II. In the Battle of the Atlantic, *Spencer* sunk the U-225 and U-175 German submarines.

The Korean War (1950-1953)

When North Korea attacked South Korea on June 25, 1950, the United States allied itself with the democratic South Korean nation. However, Coast Guard officers had been tipped off about the invasion. They were stationed at the former Japanese naval base in South Korea, training members of what would later become the South Korean Navy. During the Korean War, twenty-two cutters served at remote weather stations in the Pacific Ocean, gathering data for aircraft about approaching storms.

Long-range aids to navigation (LORAN) stations, located in the Pacific Ocean, allowed Coast Guard crews to share vital information with the other armed forces. In January 1953, the Coast Guard performed a search-and-rescue role when they learned Chinese forces shot down a US Navy reconnaissance plane.

In the United States, the Coast Guard role focused on port protection and safety. Crews checked identification and certification for merchant sailors and supervised the loading of dangerous cargo such as weapons and ammunition. During the Korean War, the Coast Guard grew to thirty-five thousand members. Broadening peacetime roles to support the other services while America was at war allowed the Coast Guard to become flexible during times of need.

UNIQUE CHALLENGES: VIETNAM TO CUBA

V ietnamese Communists were successful in repelling the French from their country in 1954, ending more than a century of colonization. They then partitioned the country into two separate states. As communism threatened to spread from North to South, the United States began sending supplies and military advisors to South Vitenam.

Small-Boat Handling in Vietnam

Once again, the Coast Guard's expert small-boat handling—particularly in shallow-water ports—helped when a coastal surveillance force was developed for riverine warfare in 1965. As military planners realized the North Vietnamese Vietcong were using rivers to ship large quantities of arms, supplies, and soldiers, shallow-water expertise was in high demand. Coast Guard boats helped detect enemy activity as nearly sixty thousand junks and sampans (boats) crossed the twelve-hundred-mile coast.[1] Intercepting all of the North Vietnamese vessels that were smuggling weapons led to "Operation Market Time," which included Coast Guard eighty-two-foot small boats with in-shore maneuverability, and weapons. The Department of Defense felt Coast Guard involvement in surveillance and coastal defense would mirror their role in the United States and improve the overall effectiveness of US naval forces.

During the first month, Division 11 boarded eleven hundred sampans, inspected more than four thousand small boats, and established blockades that improved security for South Vietnamese and American forces.[2] Coast Guard boats also provided medical evacuation, gunfire support, and transport for Special Forces troops. The Coast Guard captured enemy weapons and supplies, disrupting their operations and diminishing their capabilities, providing vital support for US naval forces.[3] Working with the Navy, the Coast Guard provided critical protection for the South Vietnam coastline, harming the enemy's efforts to resupply its forces.

Keeping Oceans Healthy

During the decades that followed, America began focusing on the passage of environmental protection laws. As such, Coast Guard missions were expanded to include environmental protection, commercial fishery protection, and marine environmental response. That created a skilled workforce ensuring the safety and health of the coastal zone. With duties ranging from patrols to documenting the health of fish species to oil-spill prevention and cleanup, Coast Guard marine-science technicians oversaw pollution response. They

During the Vietnam War, USCGC *Gresham* transported supplies and patrolled the coastline to intercept North Vietnamese weapons smugglers.

also inspected cargo and containers to ensure that environmental and safety laws were followed. They boarded ships to inspect cargo, checked containers arriving in port, and tested water samples. Their work was performed in conjunction with Coast Guard crews that check navigational signs, keep waterways running smoothly, and those that perform search and rescue.

As protectors of the coast, Coast Guardsmen and women help maintain healthy oceans, rivers, and fishery stocks. Sometimes, the Coast Guard enforces fishing regulations by boarding ships to measure the catches and to educate crew members about fishing bans and changes in regulations.

However, conservation duties date back to 1822, when Congress ordered the service to help stop the cutting of live oak trees in Florida. Crews navigated boats through winding, narrow inland waterways to stop the cutting of hardwood trees.

In 1973, the International Convention for the Prevention of Pollution by Ships set the first standard for oceans across the globe. The Coast Guard's marine environmental protection duties are vitally important to preserving healthy oceans and waterways.

On March 24, 1989, the *Exxon Valdez* ran aground, spilling more than eleven million gallons of oil into Prince William Sound in Alaska. The Coast Guard helped assist and direct an intense cleanup of more than 350 miles of coastline. The effort took more than 450 boats to and the coordination of many federal, state and local agencies over many years.[4] Skimmers and barges, cutters and aircraft were used to help in the massive environmental cleanup operation. The spill and subsequent cleanup efforts led Congress to pass the

The Coast Guard responds quickly to environmental hazards. Here, Coast Guardsmen inspect the extent of the damage to the shoreline as a result of the *Exxon Valdez* oil spill in 1989.

Oil Pollution Act in 1990, which allows the Coast Guard to enforce more strict regulations on oil tankers, owners and operators. Following the spill, the Coast Guard developed tighter controls on vessel traffic to further protect the marine environment.

During a pollution incident response, the Coast Guard generally coordinates the response for federal agencies. At the *Exxon Valdez* spill, the Coast Guard also oversaw a massive cleanup operation on the shoreline. It involved the cleaning of marine mammals and shorebirds and vessels. The lengthy operation tapped into long-standing partnerships with agencies such as the National Oceanic and Atmospheric Administration (NOAA), Environmental Protection Agency (EPA) and Department of Defense, civilian groups, state agencies, and Exxon itself.

Marine inspectors undergo training to inspect cargo and to educate commercial mariners and certain marine industries about proper container storage and how to prevent oil spills and pollution incidents. Yet pollution incidents still occur. That's why the Coast Guard mans a National Response Center where pollution incidents, oil or chemical spills or even maritime security incidents can be reported (1.800.424.8802, www.nrc.uscg,mil).

On April 20, 2010, another spill of historic proportions occurred when a deepwater oil drilling rig off the coast of Mobile, Alabama exploded. Tragically, eleven people were killed in the offshore explosion, which sent oil spewing into the Gulf of Mexico. Eighty-seven days later, the wellhead was finally capped. By then, 200 million gallons of oil had spilled into the Gulf. It had a dramatic impact on more than 16,000 miles of coastline in several states and affected many species

Coast Guard Pets

Having animals at stations and aboard ships is a time-honored military tradition. Historians say military mascots aboard ship helped control rodent infestations and provided a friendly and meaningful bond for sailors. Having a faithful pet aboard ship could also be entertaining, and allows crews to develop a shared focus and a strong bond with one another as they care for their shared pet, thus creating a common goal and improved morale.

Sinbad, a German Shepherd, lived aboard the cutter *Campbell,* and remains one of the most famous mascots in Coast Guard history. Crew members created a uniform for their mascot, a service record, and documented some of his funnier moments. There are many hilarious photos of Sinbad that can be found in books, on posters, and online. Tales of his antics were so amusing, that they were written into a book *Sinbad of the Coast Guard* by George R. Foley. A stuffed animal in his likeness was also created.

Yet other animals have also provided amusement for Coasties at sea and on land. They include:

◆ Penguin: A mascot adopted by the crew of the *Eastwind,* he often greeted the crew serving during Operation Deep Freeze I. A curious and friendly emperor penguin, he often addled up to the ship when the crew returned from patrols.

◆ Goat: Mascot of Coast Guard cutter *Perry*, he earned two awards.

◆ Bear: Mascot of the cutter *Thetis*, famous for being the largest mascot in Coast Guard history.

◆ Charlie: A California harbor seal, he barked to remind the crew he was hungry.

◆ Maximilian Talisman: A dog who was said to have served on the cutter *Klamath*, he received the United Nations medal, the Korean Service Medal, and the National Defense Service Medal.

◆ Munro: Assigned to Sector Field Office Moriches in New York, his namesake was the Coast Guard's only Medal of Honor recipient. There have been other dogs named "Munro", adopted by other crews, and each has been friendly since they are well-loved.

Chief Petty Officer Ferro, a military working dog, served in the US Coast Guard for nine years. Ferro was trained to detect explosives.

of fish and marine animals as well as shorebirds. Larger than any other spill in the United States, it was also the largest activation of Coast Guard reservists since the 9/11 attacks on the World Trade Center in New York City in 2001.

In Harm's Way in Peacetime

Coast Guard crews train constantly to hone their skills, even during peacetime. Yet working in the maritime environment can be dangerous. Homeported in Galveston, Texas, the 180-foot buoy tender *Blackthorn* had just completed an extensive shipyard overhaul in the port of Tampa, Florida, when it headed out to return home. At 8:20 P.M. on January 28, 1980, the *Blackthorn* collided with the 605-foot oil tanker SS *Capricorn* near the Sunshine Skyway Bridge in St. Petersburg, Florida. As the tanker's seven-ton anchor became embedded in *Blackthorn*, the cutter twisted and sank within ten minutes, taking twenty-three of the fifty crew members to their watery deaths.

Eventually, the *Blackthorn* was raised and towed out twenty miles off Clearwater, Florida, as part of the Pinellas County Artificial Reef Program.

While the chief mission of a buoy tender is to serve as aids to navigation, the *Blackthorn* had also been used as an icebreaker on the Great Lakes, as well as in support of various rescue and salvage operations. That included the search for survivors of National Airlines Flight 470 in February 1953.

A granite memorial commemorating the largest peacetime loss of life for the Coast Guard was dedicated on January 28, 1981. Located at the north side of the Sunshine Skyway Bridge in St. Petersburg, Florida, an annual ceremony including an honor guard and bagpipes commemorating the crew serves as a solemn reminder of the dangers facing Coast Guard crews.

Search and Rescue: The Mariel Boatlift

In April 1980, Cuban president Fidel Castro announced its Port of Mariel was open and Cubans were free to leave the country. Boarding anything that could seemingly float, nearly 125,000 Cubans migrated to the United States, often on boats crammed with too many people. More than one thousand Coast Guard vessels responded, assisted by the US Navy, for a cost of $650,000 per week between April 24 and September 22, 1980. Most of the "Marielitos", as these refugees came to be called, landed in Miami although some were sent to detention centers in Indiantown Gap, Pennsylvania; Fort McCoy, Wisconsin; and Fort Chaffee, Arkansas, for processing.

The rescue operation nearly overwhelmed Coast Guard crews, who worked to ensure the safety of the inexperienced mariners. By May, two Navy amphibious warfare ships arrived to help the Coast Guard patrol the seas, searching for capsized vessels and struggling swimmers. Each day, the Coast Guard conducted four air patrols in the waters closest to Key West, Florida, and Cuba, aided by the US Navy.

The overloaded boats, which had little safety gear, raised ongoing concerns about this mass exodus of people. On May 7, 1980, Admiral John B. Hayes held a news conference discussing the "freedom flotilla" and the safety concerns raised by the mass migration. Hayes cited the *Dr. Daniels* incident, a tug that arrived in Key West with approximately six hundred refugees on board with lifesaving equipment for only one third of the people. Concerned about a maritime

A memorial in St. Petersberg, Florida, commemorates the lives lost in the sinking of the *Blackthorn*, a tragedy that occurred during peacetime.

Cuban refugees are transported to US shores by the Florida Coast Guard during the Mariel Boatlift. Coast Guard officers saved many lives as desperate Cubans undertook hazardous journeys to America.

tragedy, he appealed to the Cuban government in the interest of safety of life at sea.

On May 10, 1980, the Coast Guard and other agencies hammered out a strategy for responding to humanitarian and legal issues raised by the influx of boats on American shores. That is when the focus shifted from search-and-rescue operations to a law enforcement mission. Using radio broadcasts, the Coast Guard announced it was illegal to transit in an unauthorized vessel and pick up people. Vessels with gross safety violations were escorted into port until violations were corrected. Commercial vessels carrying large numbers of immigrants without visas were detained. The reports from Port Mariel sounded chaotic. Refugees said the harbor had turned into a police state. At gunpoint, the vessel *Atlantis* was ordered to take 354 refugees with only eighty life-jackets aboard. That's when the Coast Guard cutter *Dallas* responded to escort the fishing vessel to its station in Key West, in Florida.

"The United States Coast Guard and the Navy have saved thousands of lives during the past seven weeks," said President Jimmy Carter. "I join every American in congratulating both organizations for their good work. We could not continue to permit this unsafe and uncontrollable flotilla to continue."[5]

In early June, the Coast Guard Commandant received presidential permission to call up reservists for up to six weeks. This historic move seamlessly integrated the work of Coast Guard reservists, active duty, and auxiliarists into a lifesaving and port security operation. By June 30, 1980, six hundred Coast Guard reservists responded from around the nation. Many Marielitos have become US citizens, and several are serving in the Coast Guard, inspired by their rescue. The sheer number of people sent by a third world country to US shores was unusual. However, it served to shape how the Coast Guard responds to mass migrations. For the Coast Guard, the Mariel Boatlift was a dramatic international event involving thousands of hours, one of the largest call-ups of reservists in peacetime, and a challenge to its resources. While migrant interdiction is often dangerous, the Coast Guard tradition of rescuing boaters in distress continues.

TWENTY-FIRST CENTURY MISSIONS

Although the Coast Guard is the smallest of the armed services, with about forty-two thousand members, it is noted for its ability to accomplish complicated tasks under extreme pressure. Nowhere was that more evident than in the ports of Boston, New York, and in Washington, D.C., when terrorists hijacked four aircraft and struck the World Trade Center and the Pentagon on September 11, 2001. After this history-changing tragedy, the Coast Guard helped secure the ports while the United States braced for more possible attacks.

The War on Terror

Coast Guardsmen were also serving overseas. In the early hours of April 24, 2004, Petty Officer Third Class Nathan Bruckenthal prepared to board a vessel off the coast of Iraq, with a crew of Navy sailors and one other Coast Guardsman. It was a trap: as they approached the vessel, it blew up. The explosion killed Bruckenthal and two Navy sailors. Since port security in the Middle East is a component of an overall plan for coastal security worldwide, the dangers crews face are part of the equation. Bruckenthal was given a stately military funeral at Arlington National Cemetery in Virginia, but his legacy inspires other brave men and women of the Coast Guard.

In the clear waters off Ash Shuaiba, Kuwait, Boatswain Mate Second Class Melissa Steinman maneuvered her boat, intently watching the horizon. Assigned to Port Security Unit 307 based in St. Petersburg, Florida, Steinman had manned the helm in Florida and Guantanamo Bay, Cuba. While the Kuwait assignment differed a bit, she understood the importance of securing foreign harbors and assuring the ports were safe and secure. Steinman and her fellow shipmates kept the watch, knowing all too well the dangers of working overseas. The loss of Coast Guardsman Nathan Bruckenthal remained painfully fresh in their minds. As the first Coast Guardsman killed since the Vietnam conflict, Bruckenthal inspired Steinman's unit and strengthened their resolve to protect safety and security at home and abroad. His death placed crews on a more heightened alert. Yet even as the Coast Guard faces shifting missions, it trains continuously to carry on the proud tradition of maritime skills including law enforcement and coastal protection.

The credible work Coast Guard crews perform has received more focused attention since terrorists struck on American soil on September 11, 2001. The entire Coast Guard has displayed admirable adaptability and flexibility, say its leaders. That is nothing new for a military organization that has changed and remolded several times during

During Operation Iraqi Freedom, US Coast Guard sentinel-class cutters were forced to fire a warning shot when an Iranian fishing boat became aggressive in the Persian Gulf.

more than two centuries of history. During Operation Iraqi Freedom, Coast Guard units provided port security for all US military operations, activating more than 68 percent of its reserve force. In late 2002, a small fleet of Coast Guard equipment—cutters, patrol boats, a buoy tender, and their crews and support teams—were deployed to the region and participated in maritime interception operations, coastal patrols, mine clearance, and search-and-rescue missions. They also maintained security for the Iraqi oil terminals in the North Arabian Gulf.

The buoy tender USCGC *Walnut* performed many important missions while deployed to the region, including a search and rescue operation for the crews of two Royal Navy helicopters that collided, and setting navigational buoys to open waterways. In addition, the commanding officers from the patrol boats *Adak, Aquidneck, Baranof,* and *Wrangell* were awarded Bronze Stars for serving as the "first line of defense" for coalition naval forces during the amphibious assault on Iraq's Al Faw Peninsula and for clearing mines within Iraqi territorial waters.

Environmental Protection

Coast Guard teams continue to learn about and train to contain oil spills to protect ocean wildlife and coastal wetlands. Through the use of highly technical instruments and staff at their renowned research and design facility in Connecticut, they can detect the origin of a spill just as you are able to link a footprint to a shoe. Careful study and gathering of evidence helps Coast Guard teams pinpoint the ship that spilled the oil, even once it has left the scene.

The Coast Guard also has a National Strike Team that can fly out to manage spills and other environmental disasters. This team was on duty when the shuttle *Columbia* broke up in January 2003 over Texas and other states. A similar team, called the Gulf Strike Team, responded to Boca Raton, Florida, in October 2001, when anthrax was detected in the American Media, Inc. (AMI) Building. Using reservist members with civilian job skills, the team from Mobile, Alabama, displayed world-class knowledge and abilities while collaborating with other environmental agencies.

Working at the Tip of the Spear: Coast Guard's "RAID" in Afghanistan[1]

Coast Guard service members have been performing a critical mission in Afghanistan (and Iraq, until combat operations ended there in 2011) as part of the "redeployment assistance and inspection detachment," or RAID. These teams are spread throughout the country and are responsible for inspecting freight containers moving in, out, and around the country. The containers hold anything from food to ammunition. When Coast Guard inspectors look at containers, some of the things they pore over are structural safety, seaworthiness, and hazardous material labeling. A long history of and specialty in effective container inspections made the Coast Guard a natural choice for this assignment. On average, RAID inspects nearly 300 containers per month and the RAID members trek to remote areas of the country with land convoys, logging an average of 35,000 miles per year. RAID is hazardous duty and many of the RAID members have been exposed to mortar attacks and direct and indirect fire.

It is the Coast Guard's duty to respond to oil spills. When the offshore oil rig *Deepwater Horizon* caught fire in the Gulf of Mexico, fire boat response crews battled the blaze.

Helping Boaters in Distress and Boater Education

The Coast Guard continues to train for and perform critical lifesaving missions referred to as search and rescue (SAR), steeped in two centuries of training and traditions. In 2013, the Coast Guard responded to 38,325 incidents and saved 3,768 lives.[2] In addition, there were 4,062 accidents, 2,620 injuries, and approximately $39 million of damages to property as a result of recreational boating accidents.[3]

By law, the Coast Guard is required to respond to boaters in distress out to twenty nautical miles at sea. However, updated technology has dramatically improved the Coast Guard's ability to receive radio transmissions-- even in poor weather and from aging radios. The ultimate goal is a safe, swift and successful rescue, and a pinpointed location of the vessel in distress helps the Coast Guard accomplish these goals.

The Coast Guard has been implementing upgrades to its communications system and also encourages boaters to use Emergency Position Indicating Radio Beacons (EPIRBs) attached to a life vest in case a vessel capsizes. Boaters can also get free vessel safety checks from the Coast Guard Auxiliary. The Auxiliary serves as the volunteer arm of the Coast Guard and has more than 32,000 members. An array of boating safety classes are offered online and in-person. Education helps boaters prepare for emergency situations until the Coast Guard arrives.

Because the Coast Guard patrols more than ninety-five thousand miles of coastline, it is prepared to juggle many missions simultaneously. While scanning the shoreline

When the Coast Guard was notified that four friends had not returned from a fishing trip, officers located the over-turned vessel and rescued the fishermen by airlift.

and ports for national security threats, crews also pay close attention to signs of boaters in distress. From the earliest days of piracy on the high seas, the Coast Guard has developed sophisticated systems of detection. These include random boat boardings that allow crews to gather information, partnerships developed with other agencies and public awareness campaigns, such as the marketing slogan, "If you see something, say something." Boaters are instructed about safety equipment such as life vests and flares. Visibility helps prevent accidents at sea and adds a measure of security to ports. Sometimes, divers and robots are used to inspect the underside of boats, bridges, and ports. Coast Guard Auxiliarists lend a uniform presence to docks and ports and their heightened visibility allows for extended coastal protection and boater safety.

Humanitarian Crisis Response

While the Coast Guard enforces safe boating practices, environmental regulations and laws, there is a true humanitarian component to the work performed. Nowhere is that more evident than in the operations aimed at rescuing migrants lost at sea. Juan Reyes recognized that important ingredient as he addressed the crew at Sector Field Office Moriches on eastern Long Island. Relaying details of a rescue at sea in 1965, Reyes gave the perspective of a nine-year-old boy sharing a small boat with thirty-three others. Poised to step aboard a Coast Guard boat for the first time in forty years, Reyes told the crews their bravery makes a difference in the lives of many. Reyes was the nine-year-old boy he spoke of and now serves as an acting associate administrator for the Environmental Protection Agency. The speech was

A family of six onboard a sinking boat off the coast of Miami, Florida, relayed Mayday distress calls. The Coast Guard responded immediately, rescuing the family just six minutes before the vessel sank and bringing them to safety onboard a Coast Guard craft.

an emotional moment for the crew and for Reyes, under-scoring the impact humanitarian service may have on someone's life.

New Organizational Structure

During the late 1700s, the Coast Guard was part of the Department of Commerce since its duties focused primarily on trade and economic stability of the young nation. In 1967, President Lyndon B. Johnson moved the Coast Guard into the Department of Transportation, although it remained one of five military branches and moved to the Department of the Navy in time of war. Protection of commerce was still a major role played by the seagoing service as it ensured the safety of marine transportation and the free flow of trade.

By 2003, expanded missions and changing global situations brought the Coast Guard even more attention in the United States. Homeland-security missions were easily folded into port security, law enforcement, marine environmental protection, and search-and-rescue missions.

It wasn't a huge surprise then when, on March 1, 2003, the Coast Guard was moved into the newly created Department of Homeland Security. The agency was created to deal with future threats to the United States. Because the Coast Guard is used to having many duties, it emerged as a beacon for the agency because it could respond so well and so rapidly to many new challenges.

Job Specialties in the Coast Guard

It takes a diverse team to run an organization like the Coast Guard. Because of its small size, efficiency is its hallmark. Behind the scenes, there are administrative functions that keep the Coast Guard running. From lawyers preparing documents to education officers ensuring education benefits are understood, the Coast Guard ensures its crews are ready to serve. Health specialists work at clinics readying crews for critical missions in the United States and overseas.

Maintaining navigational aids, meal preparation, law enforcement, radio communications, aircraft repair, drug enforcement, and boat driving are some the varied jobs

Coast Guard officers are involved in public outreach, leading tours of vessels and teaching school groups about the work accomplished by the Coast Guard.

USCG PAs are public communications experts whose job it is to raise public awareness of important Coast Guard issues. They write news releases and feature articles, shoot images and video, and answer questions from the press.

dedicated Coasties pursue. The term "shipmate" is used to describe the culture of looking out for one another. That culture is especially attractive to the children of former Coast Guardsmen and women who long to continue the legacy their parents began. It's also attractive for siblings to join the service. Chief Petty Officer Raymond Kneen is a Machinery Technician who works on engines. His sisters, Chief Petty Officer Crystalynn Kneen and Petty Officer 1st Class Sondra-Kay Kneen, work in public affairs shooting photographs and working with the media. The three active duty siblings have been stationed far from one another, but cite the Coast Guard as being their surrogate family.

Coast Guard "Chow"

Coasties serve all over the nation and the world, sometimes in remote stations. That often makes it a bit more challenging to accomplish basic tasks, such as grocery shopping for food. Many boats and some stations have galleys (kitchens) with cooks preparing meals for an entire crew, often on roiling seas. The challenge both at sea and shoreside is providing tasty, creative, and nutritious meals.

Ice cream or pizza parties help crews maintain a positive attitude on long deployments. Food-service specialists study food preparation and presentation for large groups in small galleys. This might include creating special meals for those with food restrictions. Coast Guard events often call for nautical themes, and sometimes food is presented with carrots and green peppers whittled into palm trees on small islands of lettuce and carved radishes.

While the equipment for healthy and nutritious food prep in the galleys is advancing, it is challenging to please an entire crew of people while cooking in extremely tight quarters. The term "three square meals" comes from the wooden square trays that prevented plates from sliding in stormy weather. Much of the bonding that occurs on board centers around meal and snack time, so cooks play a vital role on ships.

An important job in the Coast Guard is food service specialist. Here, Coast Guard cooks work on a meal during for the annual Military Culinary Arts Competition.

2012 Republican National Convention

While it may seem unusual for the Coast Guard to be involved in a political convention, the 2012 event had some unique security concerns that the Coast Guard was uniquely qualified to address. Held at the Tampa Bay Times Forum next to Tampa's Convention Center, the Convention venue was flanked by water. Delegates had a combination of any of thirteen bridges to cross from hotels more than twenty miles away to attend the convention. Given the high profile of the event, national security was deemed a priority. The Coast Guard undertook a meticulous planning process to create a layered waterside safety and security strategy.

A Coast Guard Response crew patrolled the waters outside the Tampa Bay Times Forum, where the 2012 Republican National Convention was held. National security was of utmost importance during this high-profile event, and the Coast Guard ensured the safety of all the convention's participants.

The convention's close proximity to the Port of Tampa and cruise ship terminals added additional challenges and safety precautions. In response, the Coast Guard partnered with local and state agencies to increase harbor patrols, performed additional recreational and commercial vessel inspections, and set waterside security zones during the convention hours. In the months leading up to the convention, security teams from various federal, state, and local agencies discussed potential threats, looking at schematics of bridges and waterways. The Coast Guard worked closely with the maritime industry, commercial and recreational fishermen, held public meetings and issued several notices to mariners to ensure the attendees and the public was aware of heightened security during the week of August 27, 2012.

National landmarks, such as the Statue of Liberty, are a constant security threat. A USCG Defender class security boat patrols New York Harbor to maintain the safety of the millions of tourists who visit the site.

SO YOU WANT TO SERVE IN THE COAST GUARD?

During times of war and from 1948 to 1973, the United States used the "draft" as a way to fill the ranks of the military. The draft required males to register for military service when they turned eighteen years old. If called up, the law obligated them to serve. Although some volunteered for service, the majority were "drafted" involuntarily. Eventually, the draft was eliminated and America adopted a policy of the "all volunteer" service.

Are You Eligible?

Military life includes wearing a uniform, adhering to dress codes, regulations, customs, and traditions. There is a long tradition and culture of respect as addressed by the Coast Guard motto "Honor, Respect and Devotion to Duty." Both enlisted and officers work in buildings, on ships and aircraft, and at small-boat stations. Coast Guard stations are found throughout the United States and its territories, although overseas assignments are available.

Requirements for applicants include:

◆ Being between seventeen and twenty-eight years of age with a high school diploma or GED

◆ Being a US citizen or resident alien

◆ Rigorous physical requirements, passing a vision and hearing exam

◆ Good scores on the Armed Forces Vocational Aptitude Battery (ASVAB) test

Recruits are sent to boot camp for eight weeks at the Coast Guard Training Center in Cape May, New Jersey, once a contract is issued and signed. The contract provides the details of pay, rate and rank, G.I. Bill education benefits, military clothing allowance, and money for housing, food, and board.

In boot camp, recruits undergo intensive physical fitness training and classroom instruction. Included in their training are courses on first aid, weapons handling, seamanship, shipboard firefighting, safety, survival in water, and nautical terminology.

Becoming an Officer

Enlisted Coast Guardsmen are eligible for promotion after they complete on-the-job training and check off qualifications that include professional military requirements and job specific duties. Biannual evaluations outline career-development paths. Once in the Coast Guard, there are several paths for promotions.

Competition for Officer Candidate School (OCS) is tough. Here are some of the requirements:

US Coast Guard Chief Petty Officer Matthew Fredrickson leads recruit training with Recruit Company India 188.

- Be between 21 and 35 years
- Meet character standards for fiscal responsibility and moral judgment
- Be a US citizen (born or naturalized)
- Have a bachelor's degree or higher
- Have a rank of E-5 or above
- Earn SAT scores of 1100 or higher or ASVAB (Armed Services Vocational Aptitude Battery) scores 109 or higher

The Creed of the Coast Guard

The Coast Guard Creed was written by Vice Admiral Harry G. Hamlet, who was commandant of the US Coast Guard from 1932 to 1936. It is known by all Coast Guardsmen.

I am proud to be a United States Coast Guardsman.

I revere that long line of expert seamen who by their devotion to duty and sacrifice of self have made it possible for me to be a member of a service honored and respected, in peace and in war, throughout the world.

I never, by work or deed, will bring reproach upon the fair name of my service, nor permit others to do so unchallenged.

I will cheerfully and willingly obey all lawful orders.

I will always be on time to relieve, and shall endeavor to do more, rather than less, than my share.

I will always be at my station, alert, and attending to my duties.

I shall, so far as I am able, bring to my seniors solutions, not problems.

I shall live joyously, but always with due regard for the rights and privileges of others.

I shall endeavor to be a model citizen in the community in which I live.

I shall sell life dearly to an enemy of my country, but give it freely to rescue those in peril.

With God's help, I shall endeavor to be one of His noblest Works . . .

A UNITED STATES COAST GUARDSMAN.[1]

The Coast Guard Academy

Founded in 1876, the Coast Guard Academy is located in New London, Connecticut. Its motto is "The sea yields to knowledge." Tuition, room, and board are free and uniforms and pay are provided. However, a five-year service obligation after graduation is required. Entrance differs a bit from the other four military service academies and requires a high grade-point average and good SAT scores as opposed to a congressional appointment for admittance.

There are six thousand applications annually for three hundred positions. Eligibility requirements include:

◆ Strong grades and competitive SAT or ACT scores
◆ Being physically fit and having good athletic skills

Cadets use a sextant to determine the sun's altitude during a celestial navigation course.

◆ Motivation and interest in leadership development

◆ Suggested SAT scores of 650 in math, 620 or higher in critical reading

For students entering their senior year of high school, the Academy Introduction Mission (AIM) program offers a five-day realistic orientation program. It allows both the student and the Academy to determine if applicants have the skill, desire, and determination to succeed in such a program. It provides competition steeped in science, boating and engineering principles, and participants say it is challenging, but fun.

Cadets spend time sailing aboard the barque *Eagle,* America's tall ship and the Coast Guard Academy's training vessel. The Academy is academically rigorous, and leadership training is progressive throughout the four years. The four-year curriculum includes marine engineering, naval architecture, marine and environmental science, government, and management. Cadets graduate with a bachelor's of science degree and a commission in the United States Coast Guard.

Part-Time Coasties

In On February 19, 1941, the Coast Guard Reserve and Auxiliary Act was passed, creating a part-time force to support and augment the Coast Guard. Reservists serve two days a month and train an additional two weeks on active duty annually. Reservists have been deployed on extended active duty to support hurricane and oil spill responses, and to support the active duty force in a variety of mission areas such as port security and law enforcement at home and overseas. The Coast Guard is authorized for about 8,600

Training on a "Barque"

Since 1947, Coast Guard Academy cadets have boarded a 295-foot, three-masted barque called the *Eagle*. A barque is a sailing vessel with at least three masts. With its twenty-three white sails, this ship is where cadets begin their training at sea. The ship was built in 1936 for cadets to train in the German Navy. America received the ship in 1946 as a war prize from Nazi Germany. With her teak wood weather decks, more than 22,000-square-feet of sail and 200 lines controlling the sails and yards, *Eagle* provides an ideal environment for navigational, for helm watches, engineering, and leadership training.

Cadets practice using a traditional navigation tool called a sextant, rigging the sails, tying knots, and swabbing the decks. During the first summer before the academic year starts, cadets have a one-week taste of seagoing tradition. Future summers include lengthier cruises with increased duties.

As a floating classroom, the majestic tall ship *Eagle* offers cadets problem-solving, critical thinking and seamanship opportunities under sail that mirror the best naval traditions.

reservists. The Reserve motto is "professionalism, patriotism and preparedness," which addresses varied missions reservists perform. Reservists provide skill and proficiency in a wide array of areas including boat handling, law enforcement, marine environmental protection, marine safety, public affairs, and administrative work.

Because the Coast Guard performs many important missions, reservists have been called for active duty missions more frequently. They have deployed in support of hurricane response and recovery efforts, helped with NASA shuttle operations, manned the helm during a bridge collapse, worked on pollution response, and supported an array of national and VIP special security events, such as the Super Bowl. From round-the-clock security patrols at ports during Operation Enduring Freedom in Afghanistan to the harbor and shore side security patrols near the military prison at Guantanamo Bay, reservists have brought an array of expertise, skills, and training to the Coast Guard.

Coastie Volunteers

The Coast Guard Auxiliary is an all-volunteer arm of the Coast Guard that also provides greater efficiency and education of the boating public. Founded in 1939, the Auxiliary is dedicated to supporting the Coast Guard through air and water patrols, teaching boating-safety courses, and educating the public. In the past decade, their skills have allowed them to take on additional roles. Auxiliarists function much like the volunteers in a hospital. They answer phones, teach courses, fly their own aircraft, or pilot their own vessels as part of a search-and-rescue mission. Their reliable, voluntary

Coast Guard reservists must train constantly to develop precision, hone their skills, and ensure readiness. Here, a Port Security crew conducts tactical boat crew training exercises at Naval Amphibious Base in Coronado, California.

Petty Officer 2nd Class Benjamin J. Kiger is a storekeeper, which means he is responsible for issuing and maintaining equipment, as well as reordering important supplies such as aircraft or boat parts.

service makes these civilians an integral and welcome part of the Coast Guard family.

Jobs in the Coast Guard

Rates describe the type of job you perform in the Coast Guard. Many Coast Guard careers have direct counterparts in the civilian (nonmilitary) world. This allows Coasties to transfer their skills to new jobs when they leave the service. A partial listing of rates is listed below:

- **Aviation Survival Technician**—Inspects, services, and repairs aircraft and provides safety training.
- **Boatswain's Mate**—Masters of seamanship service on all types of Coast Guard ships.
- **Damage Controlman**—Welds and cuts metal for repairs; fights fires; repairs plumbing, buildings, and ships; and helps detect and decontaminate chemical and biological weapons.
- **Electrician's Mate**—Installs, maintains, and repairs electrical equipment.
- **Electronics Technician**—Maintains and repairs electronics, radios, radar, computer, and navigation equipment.
- **Food-service Specialist**—Prepares food at stations and on ships.
- **Gunner's Mate**—Serves as specialists in small arms, including pistols, rifles, machine guns, and 76 mm guns.
- **Health-services Technician**—Provides healthcare services for Coasties.
- **Machinery Technician**—Operates and maintains all types of Coast Guard machinery.

◆ **Marine Science Technician**—Investigates pollution and oversees pollution cleanups; patrols harbors for safety and security; boards foreign vessels to enforce pollution and navigation laws.

◆ **Musician**—Plays in the United States Coast Guard Band.

◆ **Storekeeper**—Responsible for clothing, parts, and other supplies.

Playing Music in the Coast Guard

Formed in 1925, the United States Coast Guard Band has been one of the five premier military service bands ever since. Stationed at the Coast Guard Academy in New London, Connecticut, members are graduates of renowned music academies. One of the most respected military bands in the world, the Coast Guard band performs at such prestigious venues as the John F. Kennedy Center for the Performing Arts in Washington, D.C., and Lincoln Center and Carnegie Hall in New York City. Routinely touring throughout the United States, it has also performed overseas. The band also provides National Public Radio with recordings for broadcasts, and members have recorded CDs. The band has performed at every presidential inauguration since 1928.

Coast Guard Statistics

As of 2015, 40,446 men and women comprised the United States Coast Guard's active duty forces. An additional 8,503 reservists expand the ranks a bit, while 8,241 civilians and 29,792 Auxiliarists work for the Coast Guard filling a wide range of positions. These critical employees provide a richness and diversity of skills, background, and experience.[2]

The prestigious Coast Guard Academy band marches down
Fifth Avenue during New York City's Veterans Day Parade.

DIVERSITY IN THE COAST GUARD

Women and minorities have long made significant contributions to the Coast Guard. Changing political landscapes and economic conditions have, however, influenced their standing. However, overall, today's Coast Guard is more reflective of our diverse society.

African Americans in the Coast Guard

From the earliest days of the Revenue Cutter Service until 1843, African-American slaves were forced to serve in the Coast Guard as stewards, cooks, and seamen. In 1865, slaves were freed by the Thirteenth Amendment to the Constitution. Free African Americans also joined the Revenue Cutter Service. In 1875, the Life-Saving Service employed more than twenty-five African Americans at life-saving stations on the eastern seaboard.

The only all-black crew in the history of the Coast Guard operated Station 17 at Pea Island, North Carolina. While all were freed slaves, its keeper, Richard Etheridge, was also a decorated Civil War veteran. When an all-white crew refused to serve under his leadership, he appointed an all-black crew, all of whom saved men, women, and children in many notable and daring rescues. Etheridge planned drills to hone the skills of his lifesaving crews and they became known for rescues off the treacherous and rocky North Carolina Coast.

The crew was awarded the Gold Lifesaving Medal nearly one hundred years after the courageous rescue of all passengers aboard the *E.S. Newman*, which had run aground when a hurricane struck the Outer Banks of North Carolina. When Richard Etheridge and his crew arrived on scene, the conditions prohibited use of their rescue equipment. By ingeniously tying lines around two Pea Island crew members, the lifesavers could alternate and make eight separate swims out to the ship and rescue passengers in the pounding surf and blustery conditions. One of Etheridge's men, Theodore Meekins, having served for some forty-one years, eventually drowned during a particularly tough rescue.

In 1887, Captain Michael A. "Roaring" Healy became the only African American to command a cutter before the formal creation of the Coast Guard. From 1887 to 1895, Healy served as commanding officer of the cutter *Bear*, catching illegal seal hunters, bringing medical supplies to Alaskans, preparing navigational charts, and documenting ice and weather reports. When Healy retired, he had achieved the third-highest officer rank in the Revenue Cutter Service.

In the twentieth century, African Americans took on more and more roles in the Coast Guard. In 1945, the first

In the Pea Island Lifesaving crew, Surfman Herbert M. Collins carried out vital search-and-rescue responsibilities during World War II. The Pea Island Station was decommissioned in 1947.

five African-American women joined SPARs, a female division of the Coast Guard.

Today, African Americans are an integral part of the efficient lifesaving and security force that they helped build.

Native Americans in the Coast Guard

Since 1877, Native Americans have also served in the Coast Guard. They first comprised a lifesaving-station crew at Neah Bay, Washington. Native Americans also served in the US Lighthouse Service before the creation of the US Coast Guard. Through the twentieth and twenty-first centuries, Native Americans served at lighthouses including Point Arena, in California and Gay Head in Massachusetts.

Charles W. Vanderhoop may be the only Native American principal lighthouse keeper, when he served at Gay Head. Petty Officer Joseph R. Toahty was a member of the Pawnee Nation. As a trained coxswain, he served in landing operations at Guadalcanal and Tulagi. Both men have been credited with important rescues.

Hispanic Americans in the Coast Guard

Hispanic Americans achieved success in the Coast Guard as lighthouse keepers in the 1800s and early 1900s. They also served in the Revenue Cutter Service and the US Life-Saving Service. In 1920, Mess Attendant First Class Arthur Flores and Seaman John Gomez were awarded the Silver Lifesaving Medal for heroism for saving survivors of the schooner *Isaiah K. Stetson*, which sank off the coast of Massachusetts. Hispanic Americans continued their service through World War II and twentieth century conflicts.

MCPOG: Master Chief Vincent W. Patton, III

A native of Detroit, Michigan, Vince Patton was an Eagle Scout who aspired to serve in the sea services because his older brother served in the Navy. He joined the Coast Guard and immediately set his sights on becoming the Master Chief Petty Officer of the Coast Guard, or MCPOCG, the Coast Guard's senior enlisted leader. Almost thirty years later, he realized his goal when Master Chief Patton was selected to serve as the first African-American MCPOCG from 1998–2002.

As MCPOCG, Master Chief Patton served as the senior advisor to the Commandant of the Coast Guard and the secretaries of Transportation and Defense on

issues affecting the 40,000 active duty, reserve enlisted, and civilian personnel working for the Coast Guard. His degrees are numerous: He holds a Bachelor's of Science, a Bachelor's of Arts, a Master's of Arts, a Master's of Divinity and a Doctorate in Education. He has also run some fifteen marathons.[1]

For retired Master Chief Petty Officer Luis Diaz, a varied perspective has helped him enjoy a twenty-eight-year career. He spent twenty-two years on active duty and six years as a civilian public affairs officer in Miami, Florida. He was the first Puerto Rican to reach the ranks of chief petty officer, senior chief petty officer, and master chief petty officer. A veteran of many important military operations, including Vietnam while in the Navy, he also worked on the 1994 mass exodus of Haitian and Cuban immigrants and many hurricane recovery efforts as well as cruise ship-related operations.

Asian Americans in the Coast Guard

Asian Americans also have a history of serving their country in the US Lighthouse Service. Manuel Ferreira, a native of Maui, began his career as a lighthouse keeper with the US Lighthouse Service in 1908, retiring from the Coast Guard in 1946. He served in seven lighthouses throughout Hawaii. During World War II (from 1941 to 1945), Florence Ebersole Smith Finch, a Filipino, became the only SPAR to receive the Pacific Campaign ribbon. As part of the war effort, Finch smuggled food into the island's prison camps before being captured, beaten, and tortured in three camps. Rescued by American forces, she was one of only a handful of women to be awarded the US Medal of Freedom. Manuel Tubella Jr., was the first Filipino American aviator in the Coast Guard, and a reservist as well. In 1962, Kwang-Ping Hsu was a distinguished aviator who served for three decades.

Asian Americans in the Coast Guard continue the rich tradition started more than a hundred years ago by their ancestors in the US Lighthouse Service.

Vivien S. Crea, Vice Commandant of the Coast Guard

The first female to serve as second in command of a military service, Vice Admiral Vivien S. Crea achieved the rank of vice commandant. Her resume includes a series of "firsts": the first female air-station commander and commander, Atlantic Area and Maritime Defense

Zone, the first female presidential aide (serving under President Ronald Reagan), and the first woman to achieve flag officer status in the Coast Guard. She is one of only a few pilots to have flown the C-130 Hercules, the H-65 Dolphin helicopter, and the Gulfstream II jet.

Vice Admiral Crea earned four Legion of Merit awards, the Defense Superior Service Medal, and the Meritorious Service Medal. She holds master's degrees from Central Michigan University and the Massachusetts Institute of Technology.

Women in the Coast Guard

As early as the 1830s, women served as lighthouse keepers in the old Lighthouse Service. SPARs made important contributions to the war effort throughout World War II. Although the group was officially deactivated in 1947, the US Coast Guard Women's Volunteer Reserve began in January 1950.

In 1973, the Women's Reserve ended and women were given active-duty status in the Coast Guard. Two years later, some began to train as pilots. In 1976, the Coast Guard Academy started to admit women. It is, however, notable that in 2013, the Secretary of Defense repealed restrictions on women in combat, yet the Coast Guard had lifted barriers to women years earlier.

The Right Focus

While some milestones for women and minorities have been highlighted, the Coast Guard is successful because it taps into the varied experience, skill, jobs, and professionalism of its members and volunteers. Yet each requires the right equipment and vehicles to prepare for Coast Guard missions, whether by sea or air. Upgraded technology helps Coast Guard crews perform important missions on behalf of the American people.

In his State of the Coast Guard address in February 2015, Coast Guard Commandant Admiral Paul Zukunft reiterated the multi-mission maritime experience of the Coast Guard. Tapping into its varied background, the present-day Coast Guard continues to protect lives and property at sea, provide protection for the marine environment and secure the freedom of the seas:

When Coast Guard Academy cadets take their oath of office during commencement exercises, they officially become ensigns.

Today, the United States is already the world's largest producer of natural gas and crude oil. Industry is predicting that domestic energy production will exceed consumption by 2020. It's a trend expected to continue for at least 20 years. This is significant to me, because much of that oil and gas moves on our Nation's maritime transportation system. This is a maritime transportation system that already contributes $650 billion annually to the nation's gross domestic product and sustains more than 13 million jobs. Yes, the safety and security of our waterways are foundational to US economic prosperity.[2]

Lt. j.g. Lashanda Holmes is the first female African-American helicopter pilot in the Coast Guard. The Coast Guard is the only branch of the US military in which women can perform every job that men can.

Master Chief Leilani L. Cale-Jones, Deputy Master Chief Petty Officer of the Coast Guard

Master Chief Leilani L. Cale-Jones enlisted in the Coast Guard in July of 1987. She quickly moved up the ranks in the Coast Guard and earned a number of degrees along the way. In addition to serving as the Deputy Master Chief Petty Officer of the Coast Guard since May of 2014, she holds a Masters Certificate in Quality Systems Management and a Green Belt in Six Sigma and an MBA in Strategic Leadership. Master Chief Cale-Jones is a graduate of the Coast Guard's Leadership and Management School, Coast Guard Chief Petty Officer Academy East, the Navy's Senior Enlisted Academy and the National Defense University Command Senior Enlisted Leader Course.

Master Chief Cale-Jones' awards include the Meritorious Service Medal with two gold stars, Coast Guard Commendation Medal with two gold stars and the Operational Distinguishing Service Device, Coast Guard Achievement Medal with two gold stars, the Commandant's Letter of Commendation with one gold star, and two Antarctic Service Medals.

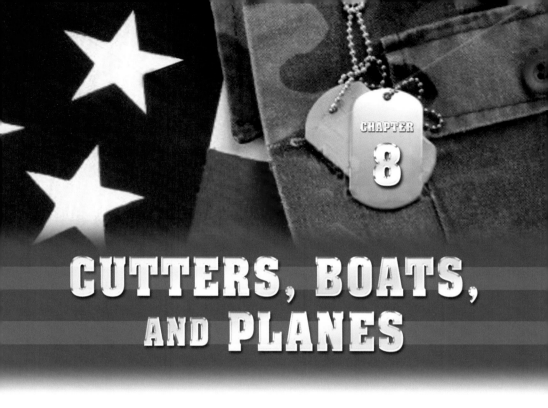

CUTTERS, BOATS, AND PLANES

Whether providing water-based support to NASA missions at Cape Canaveral or critical hurricane disaster relief in New Orleans or port security in Kuwait, the Coast Guard uses a variety of seagoing and airborne equipment to perform their varied missions, including "cutters," boats, and aircraft.[1]

Coast Guard boats include cutters, icebreakers, buoy tenders, construction tenders, patrol boats, and harbor tugs—just to name a few. Coast Guard pilots fly critical missions for the Coast Guard using both fixed wing and rotary aircraft, including C-130s, MH-60 Jayhawks, and MH-65 Dolphin helicopters. A recent addition to the Coast Guard is the Helicopter Interdiction Tactical Squadron (HITRON) unit, the Coast Guard's first and only airborne law-enforcement unit trained and authorized for the airborne use of force.

The US Coast Guard has a fleet of cutters as well as small boats. This is the first national security cutter. It can operate in conjunction with the maritime patrol aircraft *Ocean Sentry*.

The Boats Used by the US Coast Guard

The Coast Guard has a variety of boats in its arsenal, but they fall into two main categories: cutters and small boats. A "cutter" is any Coast Guard vessel sixty-five feet in length or greater, and having adequate accommodations for crew to live on board. All vessels under 65 feet in length are classified as boats and usually operate near shore and on inland waterways.

Cutters

The 378-foot High Endurance Cutter (WHEC) class are the largest cutters, except for icebreakers, ever built for the Coast Guard. They use diesel engines and gas turbines, and have controllable-pitch propellers. They are equipped with a helicopter flight deck, a retractable hangar, and the facilities to support and house a helicopter crew. They were introduced to the Coast Guard inventory in the 1960s. Highly versatile and capable of performing a variety of missions, these cutters operate throughout the world's oceans.

Icebreakers

When the RMS *Titanic* collided with an iceberg on April 15, 1912, more than fifteen hundred lives were lost at sea. That tragic loss of life immediately increased awareness of ice hazards in the ocean. Initially, the Navy assigned two ships for patrol, but then ran short on manpower. In 1914, when the Safety of Life at Sea (SOLAS) Treaty was signed by the world's great maritime powers, the Coast Guard, a natural lead agency for maintaining the safe flow of commerce, was given responsibility for ice patrol from the Chesapeake Bay to Maine. On the Great Lakes where seven navigable waterways

Icebreakers are essential to creating channels for access to military and science stations. Here, the Coast Guard Cutter *Polar Star* grooms a channel in the ice near the National Science Foundation's McMurdo Station, Antarctica.

are ordinarily filled with cargo ships, ice breaking became a priority to keep shipping channels open.

The Polar Class icebreakers are among the largest US Coast Guard cutters. Each is 399 feet long. These ships have been specifically designed for open-water icebreaking and have reinforced hulls, special icebreaking bows, and a system that makes icebreaking a lot easier to do. The *Polar Sea* and *Polar Star* were built in the 1970s. They serve science and research teams in the Arctic and Antarctic areas, as well as provide supplies to out of-the-way stations. In the polar regions, heavy icebreakers have been the only surface ships capable of creating a safe channel to resupply scientific and military stations in Antarctica and the Arctic. The Polar Class ships have also responded to oil spills and search-and-rescue cases, and they have helped expand our understanding of heavy ice and its impact on navigation. The International Ice Patrol has used aircraft to locate the boundaries of the ice field, thus saving lives and money for international shipping companies and the international field of commerce.

Training Vessels

A three-masted ship called a barque, the *Eagle* is 295 feet long and is located at the Coast Guard Academy in New London, Connecticut. It serves as a way to teach cadets traditional sailing, while providing outreach to the general public. It is one of five such training barques in the world. The others are located in Romania, Portugal, Germany, and Russia.

The *Eagle*'s name pre-dates the founding of the United States Coast Guard. The first *Eagle* was commissioned in 1792, just two years after the founding of the Revenue Marine, the forerunner of today's Coast Guard.

The barque *Eagle* serves as a training vessel for cadets. Recruits board the Coast Guard cutter and undergo five weeks of boot camp, which prepares them for careers in the US Coast Guard.

Today, the *Eagle* can serve about 175 cadets and instructors from the US Coast Guard Academy at a time. Cadets are taught seamanship on its decks.

On the teak decks and rugged rigging of the *Eagle*, male and female cadets are first confronted with sea challenges. From this experience they develop a respect for the wind, waves, and weather they will likely face in the Coast Guard. Each drill and exercise is designed to test the limits of their endurance. They learn to conquer any fear they may have. The training cadets receive on this sailing vessel has helped prepare them for their Coast Guard careers. Cadets have a chance to apply navigation and engineering training received in classes at the academy. As upper class cadets, they perform junior-officer leadership roles. As underclass cadets, they act as the crew of the *Eagle*. They watch the helm and steer the vessel using the giant brass and wood wheels. This allows them to try Coast Guard duties from all perspectives. Teamwork is imperative.

More than two hundred lines of rigging must be coordinated during a major ship maneuver, so cadets learn the name and function of each line while working in the rigging—well above the decks and often while underway. The steel hull of the *Eagle* is almost half an inch thick. The *Eagle* moves easily through water reaching a top speed of 17 knots (about 19.5 miles per hour). At the Coast Guard Academy, the *Eagle* berths on the Thames River in Connecticut. About one thousand cadets a year sail aboard the *Eagle*.

Buoy Tenders

The 175-foot Keeper-class coastal buoy tenders represent technology advances in buoy tending. All of the ships in this

Patrol boats are a cutter designed for long-distance trips. Here, a US Coast Guard Port Security Unit patrols the harbor during Operation Desert Shield.

class are named after lighthouse keepers. They are the first Coast Guard cutters that have special propulsion units instead of the standard propeller and rudder. Unlike most vessels, they can rotate 360 degrees. Combined with a thruster in the bow, the new propulsion units allow the Keeper-class cutters to maneuver in the water like never before. This is important because they need to check buoys, which help show ships safe passages through coastal waters. If the buoys are in the wrong place, a ship could hit a reef, the ocean floor, or other obstruction, possibly causing damage and endangering the lives of those on board.

The coastal buoy tenders' state-of-the-art electronics and navigation systems use a Differential Global Positioning System (GPS). As a result, these cutters maneuver and position buoys more accurately and efficiently while requiring fewer Coast Guardsmen and women to operate them.

Patrol Boats

Island-class 110-foot patrol boats are similar to a type of British patrol boat. All the boats in the Island-class boats are

GPS

Global Positioning System (GPS) is a satellite-based navigation system that was developed and operated by the US Department of Defense. It allows land, sea, and airborne users to determine their three-dimensional position, velocity, and time twenty-four hours a day, in all weather, anywhere in the world—with precision and accuracy. It is free and available to the public.

HH-65 Dolphin helicopters are used for short-range recovery missions, and are especially adept at search-and-rescue missions and polar icebreaking.

named after US islands. With the ability to go long distances, these boats replaced the older 95-foot Cape-class patrol boats. These cutters have advanced electronics and navigation equipment.

Small Boats

Small boats usually operate near shore and on inland waterways. They are smaller than cutters, ranging in size from twelve to sixty-four feet in length. They include motor lifeboats, deployable pursuit boats, and rigid hull inflatable boats.

Coast Guard Aircraft

The Guard employs more than 210 aircraft, commonly used for search-and-rescue missions, but also for law enforcement, environmental response, ice operations, and pursuit of smugglers. Coast Guard airplanes operate from air stations, while helicopters operate from flight-deck-equipped cutters, air stations, and air facilities located all over the world.

HC-130H Hercules Airplane

The Hercules is a tactical military transport aircraft. It has integrated digital controls with heads-up displays (HUDs) requiring minimal crews while offering high performance. The aircraft is used for all of the primary mission areas: long-range search and rescue, law enforcement (alien-migrant capture and counterdrug operations), airlift, and homeland security.

MH-60J/T Jayhawk Helicopter

The United States Coast Guard has forty-two medium-range Sikorsky MH-60 Jayhawk helicopters in its fleet. The Jayhawk's state-of-the-art radar, radio, and navigational

Jayhawks are medium-range helicopters.

equipment enables the helicopter to carry out search and rescue, law enforcement, military readiness, and marine environmental-protections missions.

MH-65 Dolphin Helicopter

As of August 2006, the Coast Guard had one hundred short-range HH-65A helicopters. Though normally stationed ashore, the Dolphins can be carried on board medium- and high-endurance Coast Guard cutters. They assist in the missions of search and rescue, enforcement of laws and treaties including drugs, polar icebreaking, marine environmental protection including pollution control, and military readiness. Helicopters stationed aboard icebreakers are the ship's eyes in finding thinner and more navigable ice channels. They fly reconnaissance and airlift supplies to ships and to villages isolated by winter ice. These twin-engine Dolphins can operate up to 150 miles offshore and will fly comfortably at 150 knots for about three hours.

A Coast Guard HH-60 Jayhawk helicopter conducts a training mission with a nonstandard boat.

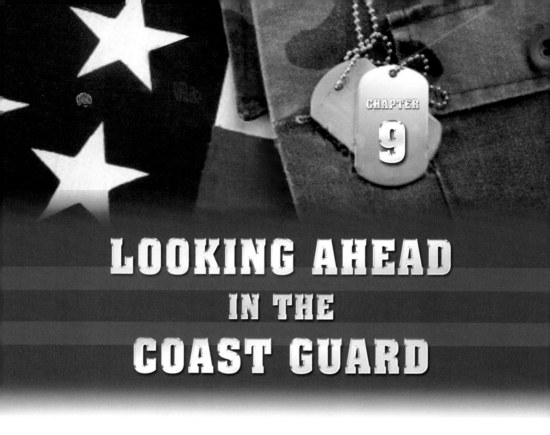

LOOKING AHEAD
IN THE
COAST GUARD

The Coast Guard protects and defends American coastal and inland waterways while ensuring the safety of our ports and protecting the flow of commerce. But the service has also been asked to combat terrorism and illegal immigrants, and to uphold environmental laws that protect marine mammals, seabirds, and fish.

The men and women of the Coast Guard work hard to prevent drug smugglers and illegal migrants from reaching American shores. Law enforcement, coastal border protection, the safe flow of commerce, and lifesaving missions all blend together to make the Coast Guard a world-renowned protector of the coast. Search-and-rescue crews are often on the lookout for homeland security threats. Using advanced technology such as underwater robots, voiceless

Coast Guard crews must be able to perform their missions in weather and surf that are often treacherous. Here, officers train to practice and maintain their skills in the heavy surf conditions notorious to the Pacific Northwest.

vessel transmissions, and advanced aircraft that can sense oil as it floats on water, today's Coast Guard is a skilled and flexible force.

Balancing America's changing security needs with protection of the marine environment and saving lives at sea has its foundations in the ever-changing needs of our country and the international community. Though more commonly known for work along the nation's 95,000 miles of coastline, the Coast Guard also works on navigable rivers and waterways and maintains safety within 360 primary ports.[1] A

Part of a security exercise, members of a Coast Guard Maritime Security Response Team fast-roped from helicopters onto the ship USS *Sisler*. The Coast Guard is continually improving and fine-tuning its training, technology, and other resources.

lengthy maritime military tradition coupled with expertise in rescue, security, and law enforcement places greater importance on Coast Guard work than ever before. The Coast Guard enforces US laws, international treaties, and maritime transportation laws as well as provides security at ports, waterways, and shore facilities. Because of this, it is the lead agency for homeland defense. The Coast Guard also leads icebreaking missions and protects the marine environment by enforcing fishery regulations, often transporting scientists to the North and South poles.

Rescue 21 Design

New missions call for new technology. Command and control systems allow the military to talk to, track, and direct units. Rescue 21 is a cutting-edge design that uses digital position tracking and allows the Coast Guard to talk directly to other first responders in an emergency. It helps the Coast Guard pinpoint the location of boaters in trouble while also allowing it to track its own boats. As of 2012, Rescue 21 covered 41,871 miles of US coastline.[2]

The Coast Guard will continue to be relied on for its expertise in search and rescue as well as law-enforcement protection of ports and other interests involving commerce. Combating terrorism, ensuring port and cargo safety, and battling drug smugglers, polluters, and illegal immigrants will all continue to pose challenges in a changing world.

Coast Guard Motto and Song

The Coast Guard motto is "Semper Paratus," meaning "Always Ready." It is also the name of the Coast Guard song, written in 1922 by Captain Francis von Boskerk while aboard

Operations specialists at Coast Guard Sector San Diego, discuss search patterns to be used in a search-and-rescue case.

the cutter *Yamacraw*. The song was updated in 1927 and again in 1969:

First Verse

From Aztec shore to Arctic zone,
To Europe and Far East,
The Flag is carried by our ships,
In times of war and peace,
And never have we struck it yet,
In spite of foe-men's might,
Who cheered our crews and cheered again,
For showing how to fight.

Chorus

We're always ready for the call,
We place our trust in Thee,
Through surf and storm and howling gale,
High shall our purpose be.
"*Semper paratus*" is our guide,
Our fame, our glory too,
To fight to save, or fight to die,
Aye! Coast Guard we are for you!

APPENDIX:
MILITARY SALARIES

Ranks, Salaries, and Insignia of Enlisted Coasties

Enlisted			
Rank	Pay Grade	Approximate Salary/month*	Insignia
Seaman Recruit	E-1	under 4 months: $1,430; over 4 months: $1546.80 per month	No insignia
Seaman Apprentice	E-2	$1,734.00	
Seaman	E-3**	$1,823.40–2,055.30	
Third Class Petty Officer	E-4	$2,019.60–2,451.60	
Second Class Petty Officer	E-5	$2,202.90–3,125.70	
First Class Petty Officer	E-6	$2,404.50–3,724.20	
Chief Petty Officer	E-7	$2,780.10–4,996.20	
Senior Chief Petty Officer	E-8	$3,999.00–5,703.60	
Master Chief Petty Officer	E-9	$4,885.20–7,584.60	

* Approximate salaries are as of 2015 and do not include food and housing allowances, free healthcare, money for college, and bonuses.

Ranks, Salaries, and Insignia of Officers

Warrant Officers			
Rank	**Pay Grade**	**Approximate Salary/ month***	**Insignia**
Chief Warrant Officer 2	W-2	$3,267.30–5,453.70	
Chief Warrant Officer 3	W-3	$3,692.40–6,477.30	
Chief Warrant Officer 4	W-4	$4,043.40–7,531.80	
Officers			
Ensign	O-1	$2,934.30–3,692.10	
Lieutenant, junior grade	O-2	$3,380.70–4,678.50	
Lieutenant	O-3	$3,912.60–6,365.40	
Lieutenant Commander	O-4	$4,449.90–7,430.10	
Commander	O-5	$5,157.60–8,762.40	
Captain	O-6	$6,186.60–10,952.40	
Rear Admiral (lower half)	O-7	$8,264.40–12,347.70	
Rear Admiral (upper half)	O-8	$9,946.20–14,338.50	
Vice Admiral	O-9	$14,056.80-17,436.90	
Admiral	O-10	$16,072.20–19,762.50	

* Salaries are as of 2015 and do not include food and housing allowances, free healthcare, money for college, and bonuses; also, an approximate salary range has been given for each rank.

TIMELINE

1716—British colonists begin building lighthouses in America.

AUGUST 4, 1790—At the prompting of Secretary of the Treasury Alexander Hamilton, the first version of the US Coast Guard, the Revenue Cutter Service, is created by a tariff act.

MARCH 21, 1791—Hopley Yeaton becomes the first commissioned officer of the Revenue Cutter Service after being appointed by President George Washington.

1798–1800—Coast Guard participates in the Quasi War with France, during which the *Pickering* captured ten enemy chips.

1808–1865—Revenue Cutter Service combats the illegal slave trade.

1812–1815—War of 1812.

JUNE 12, 1813—Revenue Cutter Service ship *Surveyor* is captured by the British frigate *Narcissus*.

1822—Helps enforce ban on the cutting of live oak trees in Florida.

1832—Secretary of the Treasury Louis McLane orders Revenue Cutter Service to assist mariners during the winter.

1836–1839—Revenue Cutter Service aids in the fight against Seminole Indians in Florida.

1837—Lifesaving becomes the core mission of the Revenue Cutter Service.

1843—African-American slaves are no longer forced to serve in the Coast Guard.

1846–1848—The Revenue Cutter Service assists the US Marine Corps in ship-to-shore battles during the Mexican-American War.

1848—Volunteer lifesaving stations are present on the Atlantic and Pacific coasts, the Gulf of Mexico coast, and the coasts of the Great Lakes.

1854—US government begins paying Life-Saving Service station keepers.

1861–1865—The American Civil War.

APRIL 11, 1861—The cutter *Harriet Lane* fires first maritime shots in Civil War.

1871—Sumner Kimball becomes chief of the Revenue Marine Service and the first superintendent of the Life-Saving Service.

1876—Academy is founded for the Revenue Cutter Service; it will become the Coast Guard Academy.

1878—The Life-Saving Service becomes independent from the Revenue Cutter Service.

1879—Ida Lewis becomes the official lighthouse keeper for the Lime Rock Lighthouse in Newport, Rhode Island.

1895—Captain Ellsworth Price Bertholf becomes first Revenue Cutter officer to attend the Naval War College.

1896—The all-African-American Pea Island crew distinguishes itself in the rescue of the *E.S. Newman*.

1898—Revenue Cutter Service helps with blockading and lifesaving efforts during the Spanish-American War.

1911—Ellsworth Price Bertholf named commandant of Revenue Cutter Service.

1915—Life-Saving Service and Revenue Cutter Service are combined to become the US Coast Guard on January 28; Ellsworth Price Bertholf is appointed first commandant of the US Coast Guard; there are 285 Life-Saving Service stations around the United States.

1917–1918—Coast Guard escorts American vessels during World War I.

1920s—Helps fight illegal alcohol traffickers during Prohibition; Coast Guard aviation program expands.

1925—Coast Guard Band is founded.

1926—Coast Guard builds its first icebreakers.

1928—Coast Guard Band performs at its first presidential inauguration.

1932—New Coast Guard Academy is built in New London, Connecticut.

1935–1941—Coast Guard helps enforce Neutrality Act.

1937—US Lighthouse Service officially becomes part of the US Coast Guard.

1939—The Coast Guard Reserve and Auxiliary are created. December 7, 1941—Coast Guard helps defend against Pearl Harbor attack.

1941–1945—World War II.

1943—The Coast Guard women's reserve, SPAR, is created.

1945—The first five African-American women join SPAR.

1947—The barque *Eagle* is acquired, and is used to train Coast Guard Academy cadets to this day.

1950–1953—Coast Guard offers combat support during Korean War.

1965–1973—Helps patrol rivers and coastlines during the Vietnam War.

1967—Moves from Department of Commerce to Department of Transportation.

Timeline

1973—Women are given active-duty status in the Coast Guard.

JANUARY 28, 1980—*Blackthorn* collides with an oil tanker, killing twenty-three Coast Guard crew members.

APRIL–OCTOBER 1980—Coast Guard provides security and lifesaving services during the Mariel Boatlift.

1989—Assists in the cleanup of the *Exxon Valdez* oil spill.

SEPTEMBER 11, 2001—Assists with marine and port security immediately after the September 11 attacks.

2003—On March 1, moves from Department of Transportation to become part of the newly created Department of Homeland Security; more than fifty-one hundred lives saved by Coast Guard teams.

2004—Petty Officer Third Class Nathan Bruckenthal becomes the first Coastie killed since the Vietnam War; Coast Guard helps in relief effort during a busy hurricane season.

AUGUST–SEPTEMBER 2005—Provides search-and-rescue and security services during and in the aftermath of Hurricane Katrina.

2010—The Secretary of Defense repeals the ban on homosexuals in the military, allowing gays to openly serve in all services.

2013—The Secretary of Defense repeals the restrictions on women in combat, opening up thousands of positions in the military.

APRIL 1, 2015—Coast Guard establishes a new rating: Diver.

CHAPTER NOTES

CHAPTER 1   Hovering Helpers

1. Memmott, Mark. "Coast Guard Rescues 14 Force by Sandy to Abandon Tall Ship," National Public Radio, October 30, 2012.
2. US Department of Security, US Coast Guard SAR Statistics, http://www.uscg.mil/hq/cg5/cg534/SAR_facts_reports.asp.
3. Personal interview with Petty Officer Josh Mitcheltree, March 1, 2006.
4. Ibid.
5. Ibid.

CHAPTER 2   Two Centuries, Many Missions

1. Alexander Hamilton, *The Federalist Papers: The Federalist No. 12*, The University of Oklahoma: College of Law, November 27, 1787, <http://www.law.ou.edu/hist/federalist/federalist-10-19/federalist.12.shtml> (October 23, 2006).
2. "Historical Chronology," *US Coast Guard*, n.d., <http://www.uscg.mil/hq/g-cp/comrel/factfile/Factcards/HistoricalChronology.html> (October 23, 2006).
3. "Surveyor, 1807," *US Coast Guard*, May 2004, <http://www.uscg.mil/history/webcutters/surveyor%5F1807.html> (November 29, 2006).
4. *US Coast Guard History*, <http://www.uscg.mil/history/h%5Fuslss.html> (December 2005).
5. "Ida Lewis," *US Coast Guard*, January 2001, <http://www.uscg.mil/history/Ida%20Lewis%20Bio.html> (October 23, 2006).

CHAPTER 3   Changing With the Times

1. Woodrow Wilson, "Primary Documents: US Declaration of War with Germany, 2 April 1917," *First World War.com*, April 14, 2002, <http://www.firstworldwar.com/source/usawardeclaration.htm> (October 24, 2006).
2. "Tampa History," *US Coast Guard*, <http://www.uscg.mil/history/Tampa_1912.html> (August 4, 2006).

3. "The Coast Guard at War: National Security & Military Preparedness," *US Coast Guard*. <http://www.uscg.mil/history/h_militaryindex.html> (October 4, 2006).

4. Kay M. Sheppard, "The Coastland Times," RootsWeb, 2004, <http://www.rootsweb.com/~nccurrit/obits/ coastlandtimes.htm> (October 24, 2006).

5. "A History of Coast Guard Aviation: The Early Years (1915–1938)," *Coast Guard Aviation History*, 2003–2006, <http://uscgaviationhistory.aoptero.org/ history01.html> (October 24, 2006).

6. "Neutrality Acts 1935–1941," January 21, 2000, <http://history.acusd.edu/gen/WW2timeline/ neutralityacts.html> (October 24, 2006).

7. "Medal of Honor Inscription," *US Coast Guard*, n.d., <http://www.uscg.mil/history/Munro%20Index.html> (August 4, 2006).

8. Dr. Robert M. Browning, Jr., "The Coast Guard at Iwo Jima," *US Coast Guard*, n.d., <http://www.uscg.mil/history/IwoJima.html> (August 4, 2006).

9. Judith Silverstein, "Adrift," *US Coast Guard: District 11 Public Affairs*, n.d., <http://www.uscgsanfrancisco.com/go/doc/586/89781/?printerfriendly=1> (October 24, 2006).

10. Brent Hurd, "America Remembers Unsung Heroes on Memorial Day," *Voice of America News*, May 31, 2005, <https://www.veteransadvantage.com/news/archive/AmericaRemembersUnsungHeroesOnMemorialDay.html> (October 24, 2006).

CHAPTER 4 Unique Challenges: Vietnam to Cuba

1. Jonathan S. Wiarda, "The US Coast Guard in Vietnam: Achieving Success in a Difficult War," *Naval War College Review*, Spring 1998, vol. LI, no. 2, <http://www.nwc.navy.mil/press/Review/1998/spring/art3-sp8.htm> (October 30, 2006).

2. Eugene N. Tulich, "The United States Coast Guard in South East Asia During the Vietnam Conflict," *US Coast Guard*, April 1998, <http://www.uscg.mil/history/h_tulichvietnam.html> (October 30, 2006).

3. Jonathan S. Wiarda, "The US Coast Guard in Vietnam: Achieving Success in a Difficult War."

4. Donald Canney, "The Coast Guard and the Environment," *US Coast Guard*, October 2000, <http://www.uscg.mil/history/h_environment.html> (October 20, 2006).

5. PA3 Judy L. Silverstein, MSO Tampa, "Memories of Mariel: 20 Years Later," *US Coast Guard*, n.d., <http://www.uscg.mil/reservist/mag2000/apr2000/mariel.htm> (November 29, 2006).

CHAPTER 5   Twenty-First Century Missions

1. Lt. Cdr. Ken G. Sieg, USCGR. "Tip of the Spear: The US Coast Guard's RAID in Afghanistan," www.army.mil, May 2, 2013.

2. US Department of Transportation, US Coast Guard 2013 Search and Rescue Statistics, http://www.rita.dot.gov/bts/sites/rita.dot.gov.bts/files/publications/national_transportation_statistics/html/table_02_49.html.

3. 2013 US Coast Guard Boating Safety Statistics: http://www.uscgboating.org/library/accident-statistics/2013ReportRevised.pdf.

CHAPTER 6   So You Want to Serve in the Coast Guard?

1. VADM Harry G. Hamlet, USCG, "Creed of the United States Coast Guardsman," *US Coast Guard*, December 1997, <http://www.uscg.mil/history/faqs/creed.html> (January 31, 2007).

2. Coast Guard Snapshot 2012, http://www.uscg.mil/top/about/doc/uscg_snapshot.pdf.

CHAPTER 7   Diversity in the Coast Guard

1. Williams, Rudi. "Coast Guard's 'Master Chief' Calculates Climb to Top," American Forces Press Service, February 10, 2000.

2. Coast Guard Commandant's 2015 State of the Coast Guard, February 2015, http://www.uscg.mil/coastguard2015/.

CHAPTER 8   Cutters, Boats, and Planes

1. Department of Homeland Security, US Coast Guard: Aircraft, Boats, and Cutters http://www.uscg.mil/datasheet/25rbs.asp.

CHAPTER 9   Looking Ahead in the Coast Guard

1. US Coast Guard Rescue 21 Program, http://www.uscg.mil/acquisition/rescue21/.

2. Ibid.

GLOSSARY

barque—A three-masted sailing vessel.

bow—The front, or pointy end, of a boat.

bridge—Control room for an engine-powered ship, and place from which the ship is steered.

charts—Maps.

coxswain—Enlisted person in charge of a boat.

cutter—A vessel that is 65 feet or longer with accommodations for the crew.

deck—Nautical term for floor.

dog—Name for a handle that opens and closes a hatch or door (hatch), as in "Dog the hatch."

flare—Safety device that can be lit so you can be seen, if in trouble.

galley—Ship's kitchen.

helm—The wheel or tiller that controls the rudder.

homeported—City where a military ship is based.

hull—The main shell of a vessel.

knot—How speed is measured at sea.

ladder—On a ship, all stairs are called ladders

mess—A group that live or work together on a ship (e.g., Chief Petty Officer's Mess). It also refers to the meal itself or food in general or the area where food is eaten. (I'll meet you on the Mess Deck)

monkey's Fist—a ball of woven lone sometimes weighted with lead.

petty officer—Enlisted men and women who are specially trained and rated.

rudder—A board-shaped piece attached to the back of a ship or boat for steering and maneuvering.

schooner—sailing vessel with two or more masts.

FURTHER READING

Books

Benson, Tyler. *The Adventures of Onyx and the Guardians of the Straits (The Adventures of Onyx)*. Gloucester, Va.: Ensign Benson Books, 2014.

Davis, Susan Page. *Always Ready*. Seattle: Amazon Digital Services, 2012.

Helvarg, David. *Rescue Warriors: The US Coast Guard, America's Forgotten Heroes*. New York: St. Martine's Griffin, 2010.

Holtkamp, Tido. *A Perfect Lady: A Pictorial History of the US Coast Guard Barque Eagle*. Mystic, Conn.: Flat Hammock Press, 2011.

Thompson, Kalee. *Deadliest Sea: The Untold Story Behind the Greatest Rescue in Coast Guard History*. New York: William Morrow, 2011.

Tongias, Michael, and Casey Sherman. *The Finest Hours: The True Story of the US Coast Guard's Most Daring Sea Rescue*. New York: Scribner, 2010.

Williams, Gary. *Guardian of Guadalcanal: The World War II Story of Douglas A. Munro, United States Coast Guard*. Westchester, Ohio: Lakota Press, 2014.

Zuckoff, Michael. *Frozen in Time: An Epic Story of Survival and a Modern Quest for Lost Heroes of World War II*. New York: Harper Perennial, 2014.

Web Sites

uscg.mil/default.asp
> Visit the official site of the US Coast Guard.

uslhs.org/
> The United States Lighthouse Society is dedicated to preserving and sharing the legacy of US lighthouses.

gocoastguard.com/
> Interested in a career in the US Coast Guard? Check the US Coast Guard Recruiting Web site.

Movies

The Perfect Storm. Directed by Wolfgang Peterson. Burbank, Calif.: Warner Bros. Pictures, 2000.
> This movie depicts the true story of a commercial fishing vessel lost at sea.

White Squall. Directed by Ridley Scott. Burbank, Calif.: Hollywood Pictures, 1996.
> Members of a sailing school fight for their lives when their ship is threatened by a white squall.

INDEX

Index

O

Officer Candidate School (OCS), 72–73
Oil Pollution Act (1990), 43
Operation Market Time, 39

P

patrol boats, 55–56, 95, 103, 105
Patton, Vincent W., III, 88
Pea Island crew, 85
Pearl Harbor, 29–30
piracy, 14–15, 17, 19, 27, 61
Polar Class icebreaker, 99
port security, 14, 37

Q

Quasi War, 17, 19

R

Reagan, Ronald, 90
Republican National Convention, Tampa, 67, 69
redeployment assistance and inspection detachment (RAID), 57
refugee rescue, 48, 51–52
Rescue 21 program, 111
rescue swimmer, 6, 8–9, 11, 13
Resnick, Bob, 30, 32
Revenue Cutter Service, 15, 17, 19, 20, 22, 25, 84–85, 87
Revolutionary War, 14–15, 17
Reyes, Juan, 61, 63
Rosenthal, Joe, 32
Ruhl, William, 32

S

Safety of Life at Sea Treaty (SOLAS), 97, 99
Scammell, Alexander, 17
search and rescue (SAR), 5–6, 13, 18, 27, 30, 32, 37, 41, 48, 51–52, 55–56, 59, 63, 78, 81, 99, 105–106, 108–109, 111
Seminole Indian Wars, 21, 25
September 11, 2001, 47, 53–56

Sinbad of the Coast Guard, 44
small-boats, 38–39, 61, 72, 78, 97, 105
Spanish-American War, 25
SPAR, 32, 34, 87, 89, 91
Steinman, Melissa, 54
Strike Teams, 56, 63

T

Tariff Act of 1790, 15, 17
terrorism, 108, 111
Titanic, RMS, 20, 97
Todd, Daniel, 6
Truman, Harry S., 37
Tubella, Manuel Jr., 89

U

U-boats, 32
US Life-Saving Service, 87
US Lighthouse Service, 18, 87, 89, 91
US Marine Corps, 25, 30
US Navy, 14, 17, 19, 25–26, 29–30, 37, 39, 48, 51, 53–54, 63, 88–89, 94, 97

V

Vietnam War, 38–39, 54, 89
Vigilant, USS, 17, 19
von Boskerk, Francis, 111, 113

W

War of 1812, 19
War on Terror, 53–56
Washington, George, 17
Wilson, Woodrow, 22, 25–27
World War I, 26–27
World War II, 29–30, 32, 34, 87, 89, 91

Y

Yeaton, Hopley, 17

Z

Zukunft, Paul, 91–92